Mindfulness
for
Compassionate
Living

Mindfulness
for
Compassionate
Living

Mindful ways to less stress
and more kindness

Dr Patrizia Collard

An Hachette UK Company
www.hachette.co.uk

First published in Great Britain in 2014 by Gaia Books,
a division of Octopus Publishing Group Ltd
Endeavour House, 189 Shaftesbury Avenue, London WC2H 8JY
www.octopusbooks.co.uk

ISBN 978 1 85675 340 1
A CIP catalogue record for this book is available from the
British Library.

Printed and bound in Hong Kong
10 9 8 7 6 5 4 3 2 1

Publisher Liz Dean
Senior Art Editor Juliette Norsworthy
Designer Joanna MacGregor
Illustrations Abigail Read
Picture Research Manager Giulia Hetherington
Assistant Production Manager Caroline Alberti

Any information given in this book is not intended to be taken
as a replacement for medical advice. Any person with a condition
requiring medical attention should consult a qualified practitioner
or therapist.

The symbol of the lotus flower is a visual
description of compassion. A beautiful
flower that grows out of the mud stands for
a beautiful mind, heart and brain growing
out of the human condition.

Contents

Introduction

When I attended my first Metta (loving kindness) retreat ten years ago, one of my most learned teachers said that self-compassion was the key to resolving all destructive emotions. When I asked her how it related to mindfulness, my special field of interest, she explained that the two belonged intrinsically together. Like Yin and Yang, compassion is an important skill, which adds to mindfulness the ability to 'love what is' and to see yourself as if you are a beautiful diamond that just needs a little polishing here and there.

So for the last eight years I have been observing how compassion training has developed in different fields such as medicine and psychotherapy, and how academic publications on the subject of compassion and loving kindness have increased year by year.

During the last decade, scientists and psychotherapists have been conducting research into 'the science of compassion'. They are attempting to identify the nature and origins of empathic, non-selfish behaviour towards others. Presently, tools are being developed that will be able to measure people's empathy, compassion and selflessness. In future, these tools will help us assess the effectiveness of any skills training that is offered for increasing self-love and compassion.

Many books published on this topic use the symbol of the lotus flower to represent compassion. A beautiful flower that grows out of the mud stands for a beautiful mind, heart and brain growing out of the human condition, which more often than not encompasses negativity, evil acts and selfishness.

Where does compassion reside and how can you cultivate it? I hope that this book will become a little treasure chest for you, where you can find new ideas and wisdom for embracing compassion, and particularly self-compassion, more deeply. It will take us on a journey, looking at Darwin's theory of 'the survival of the fittest' and how often this is not mirrored in nature. We will also pass through ancient spiritual wisdom and see what we can learn from that source. The spiritual teachers who once had the power to affect the individual – Christ and Buddha, for example – challenged us to be awake and fully alive, just as much as practising compassion and love in action. The ones who followed during the last century, such as Gandhi, Martin Luther King and His Holiness the 14th Dalai Lama, portrayed strength in character and vision and yet fully embodied self-compassion. Without the latter, it is much harder to live compassionately and care for others and the environment. When we have genuine self-love, we can tap into our true goodness, see the gifts we have been given and then experience the joy of sharing them with others.

We will open our heart to fairy tales, real-life stories, parables and poetry, and collect insights for our quest. Finally, we will look at why we need compassion more than ever now in this time of turmoil and narcissism.

Let us open our heart to fairy tales, real-life stories, parables and poetry, and collect insights for our quest

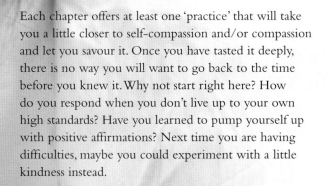

Each chapter offers at least one 'practice' that will take you a little closer to self-compassion and/or compassion and let you savour it. Once you have tasted it deeply, there is no way you will want to go back to the time before you knew it. Why not start right here? How do you respond when you don't live up to your own high standards? Have you learned to pump yourself up with positive affirmations? Next time you are having difficulties, maybe you could experiment with a little kindness instead.

Self-compassion – the ability to treat oneself kindly and without judgement when things go badly – may be more important than self-esteem for promoting feelings of well-being, according to a study published in the American Psychological Association's *Journal of Personality and Social Psychology* (2007; 92(5), 887–904). Social scientists have previously placed emphasis on how self-esteem – the ability to believe positively in oneself and to feel valued by others – creates feelings of well-being. In contrast, self-compassion involves *caring* for oneself rather than believing in oneself.

Self-compassion consists of three components: self-kindness, common humanity and mindful acceptance. While many people with high self-esteem are also self-compassionate, not all of them are. Self-compassion, in contrast to self-esteem, may be a key to maintaining resilience in the face of adversity. As Mark R. Leary, Professor of Psychology and Neuroscience at Duke University, North Carolina, has said, 'If people learn only to feel better about themselves but continue to beat themselves up when they fail or make mistakes, they will be unable to cope without defence when meeting their difficulties'.

You will need a practice journal. Find a notebook that you can either draw on or cover with photos or stickers, or just choose a lovely design that inspires you to look at the book and read and use it regularly. As we want to sow the seeds of compassion, this notebook will be your flowerbed where the first plants symbolizing your self-compassion will grow. It will guide, enrich and inspire you not to give up even when you are going through a rough patch in your life.

Before your first practice, write down on the opening pages why you want to discover and develop compassion and self-love. What has led you to begin this journey?

There is some kiss we want

There is some kiss we want
with all our lives,
the touch of Spirit on the body.
Seawater begs the pearl
To break its shell.
At night, I open my window
and ask the moon to come
and press her face against mine,
breathe into me.
Close the language door
and open the love window.
The moon won't use the door,
only the window.
There is some kiss we want
with all our lives.

Jalal al-Din Rumi
(1207-1273)

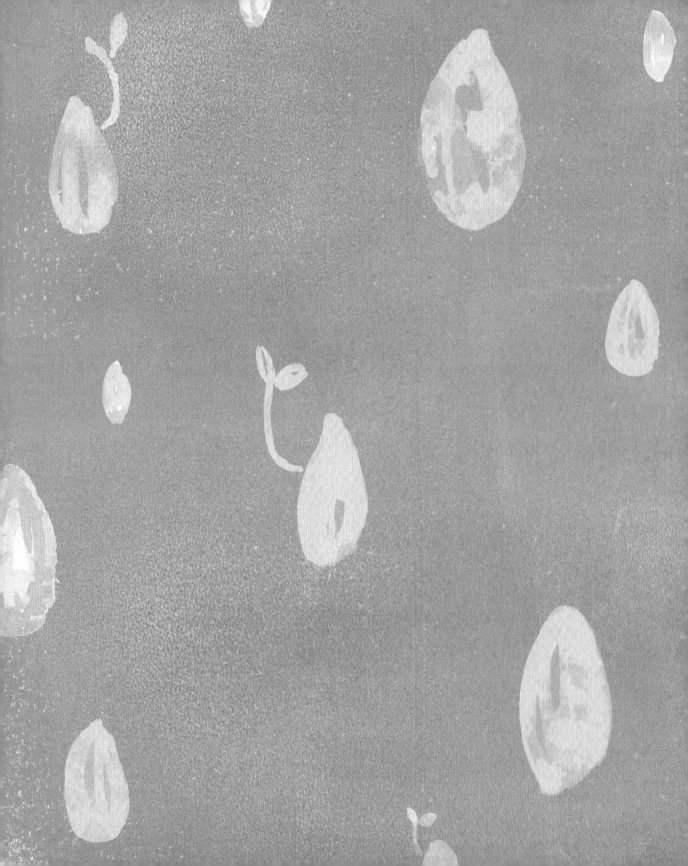

1 Planting the seeds of self-compassion

Compassion is something that everybody needs and deserves and it includes the compassion we give ourselves.

Sharon Salzberg (meditation teacher) (1952–)

MY MEMORY OF THE BIRTH of my brother is somewhat vague, but I know I was told to be kind and gentle to him. When he was just six months old, I took a huge ball of chocolate from the Christmas tree and stuffed it into his mouth. Temporarily, he was silent and sucked on my gift. Soon he began to whimper rather than cry (his mouth was too full for that) and I just watched him.

My mother passed by and, realizing something was wrong, fished my gift out of his mouth. She was not sure what my real motives had been (neither was I), but explained to me that kindness was something you offer to somebody in order to make them feel better.

I am not sure that I wanted to be kind to him; after all, he was the new baby, held by mum most of the time. Although I was barely two years old, I nevertheless had a clear emotional understanding of what kindness meant. For me, kindness was an experience that made me feel good, wanted, accepted and loved.

Compassion is a skill we can learn (thank goodness). By engaging repeatedly with a number of the exercises in this book, the area in your brain that is activated by practising compassion will actually grow, as you will read later on.

Emotional healing

Self-compassion can be the basis for emotional healing in many ways. Start by bringing your awareness to this moment, do not dwell on the past and let go of fears regarding the future. When you are totally mindful in this moment (where your life is actually happening), you may notice a number of difficult emotions, such as self-doubt, lack of direction, anxiety, anger, sadness, loneliness, shame and self-doubt. Do not judge yourself in any way for having these emotions because they are part of our human experience. Acknowledge what you find and respond as best as you can to any challenge with kindness, patience and understanding. Remember, life changes all the time and this moment will also pass, sooner or later.

Compassion towards all, on the other hand, was described thus by the mystic Thomas Merton just hours before he died: 'The whole idea of compassion is based on a keen awareness of interdependence of these living beings, which are all part of one another and all involved in one another.'

Mindful self-compassion can be developed by anyone. It is the practice of repeatedly bringing kindness and goodwill towards ourselves, especially when we are suffering, just as we would for others we care for when they are down and lost.

When we look at the need for peace in the world, it seems an impossible goal: there are wars on several continents, the balance of our environment seems to get more and more out of control, and individuals, too, aggressively choose to control or even take others' lives. We need to survive sanely in this frantic world, and that can seem unattainable. The entire insight upon which compassion is based is that the other is not the other; and that I am not I. In other words, in loving others I am loving myself and, indeed am involved in my own best and biggest and fullest self-interest. It is my pleasure to be involved in the relief of the pain of others, a pain that is also my pain. Today, an even more pressing need exists for recognizing how compassion is in everyone's best interests, and that is the issue of the survival of our common global village – loving others who are different from ourselves. It is loving ourselves while we love others. It is loving the possibilities of love and survival. It is one love that permeates all.

Mindfulness will help us patiently revisit those areas in our lives where stillness and peace are lacking. Mindfulness also teaches us to repeat meditative exercises patiently and start afresh moment by moment, even if we have slipped.

Human kindness

The literal meaning of the word compassion is 'suffering with'. Paul Gilbert (a leading British psychologist, who was awarded an MBE for his work on applied compassion for people with severe mental illness) defines it in essence as basic human kindness, with 'a deep awareness of the suffering of oneself and of other living beings, coupled with a wish and an effort to relieve it'.

If you look at children and how they worry about their pet's pain, or at a mother deeply moved by her baby's crying, you get an idea of what compassion feels like. When this occurs, you usually sense a churning in your heart and the longing to help the one who is suffering.

True compassion also shows benevolence – kind understanding rather than harsh criticism when others make mistakes – you understand that this is the human condition without applied compassion. We all fail sometimes and get it wrong.

In a 2011 article in *The New York Times,* David Brooks drew attention to Darwin's theory of the survival of the fittest. Only the strong species have a chance to survive and they need not only to be strong but also self-obsessed, or at least self-serving. Humans are a brilliant example of self-centredness. Brooks argues that *Homo sapiens* fights for status, a good lifestyle and, of course, an attractive partner. Every so often, however, one hears stories that do not fit into this definition of self-absorption. Scientists, evolutionary psychologists and neuroscientists are conducting more and more scientific research into empathy, compassion and teamwork.

Even when focusing mainly on our own needs and wants, we do have motivation to reward kind-heartedness with kindness. We do it so that we can expect help when we are down or in trouble. People usually remember generosity, and feel drawn to work with others who are kind.

There is no doubt that interrelated groups thrive better. Cooperation is as important for progression as evolution. Michael Tomasello, the author of *Why We Cooperate*, discovered that children will assist others and exchange information. He tried the same tests with chimpanzees who, at a similar age, did not act in such a way. Toddlers were prepared to share food with strangers; the apes were not. Tomasello claims that a 14-month-old child who observes grown-ups having difficulty will attempt to help, unlike his chimpanzee counterpart. Thus we can conclude that the human mind developed differently from that of the other primates. We can – and do – cooperate. In his book *The Righteous Mind,* Jonathan Haidt argues that we are 'the giraffes of altruism'. Just as giraffes grew longer necks to help them survive, human minds evolved to include morality to help them succeed.

When we experience trauma, we often tend to criticize ourselves ('typical, this kind of thing would only happen to me') and recoil and isolate ourselves from the world because we feel tainted. Kristin Neff, a Professor in human development and culture at the University of Texas, and Christopher Germer, a clinical psychologist, believe that self-compassion can help us to heal and leave behind the physical and emotional wounds that the traumatic experience has caused. They recommend 'self-kindness', understanding that while negative emotions can – and will – be there for a time, eventually everything will change.

When I worked for Amnesty International, I came across reports of prisoners who had experienced torture. It was notable that Tibetans seemed to have considerably fewer individuals suffering from post-traumatic stress disorder. When interviewed, several shared their common belief: of course, they were deeply wounded about what other humans had done to them. What was worse, however, was contemplating how much their torturers must suffer every time they remembered their terrible actions.

Practice: Compassionate writing

Many of us feel unhappy about our looks, abilities
or aptitudes at some time or another. Here is an
opportunity to be 'irrational', let go of frustrations
and experience the perspective of self-compassion.

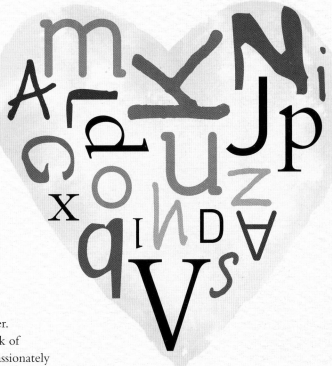

1   Write down everything you feel about
    your 'imperfections' in a letter to yourself.
    Let it all come to the surface. If you need
    to use strong language or vent your
    anger, feel free!

2   Visualize someone who truly cares for
    you. (If you find visualizing difficult,
    just picture their name written on your
    heart.) How would this person respond
    if you read your letter to them? Imagine
    this friend loving you unconditionally,
    seeing you as you truly are. How might
    they respond, in words and deeds? Try to be
    real – this friend truly knows you and would
    tell you if they thought you had engaged in
    harmful actions.

3   Now write a response to yourself from your
    friend's perspective, again in the form of a letter.
    Move into the sensitivity of your friend – think of
    everything they might mention, as they compassionately
    hold you in kindly awareness, warmth and acceptance and
    with a genuine intention to help you, and just loving you for
    who you are.

4   Read and re-read the letter and feel your heart respond to this compassion
    and kindness. What does it feel like – what words or phrases spring to mind?
    This is a taste of self-compassion.

5   Read your letter whenever you feel that your levels of self-criticism are
    escalating. When you cannot do this, simply remember the feeling of
    self-compassion you experienced when you last read the letter.

Practice: Feeling the music

This practice was inspired by my fellow trainer and teacher Helen Stephenson as she recalled a Quaker meeting she once attended. (Even though here the higher self is referred to as 'God', if you follow another principle of spirituality or your own personal higher self, the practice may still help you.)

When you go before God in prayer you cannot leave anything behind. You carry in this moment every person, every incident, every thought, every feeling you have ever had and as you lay yourself before God so you bring all the mess as well. 'My prayer', she said, 'is really one sentence: Here I am, what a mess.'

Mother Mary Clare of the Sisters of Love of God, as quoted by Jack Nicholls in *Struggling to be Holy* **by Judy Hirst (Darton, Longman and Todd, 2008)**

Father Jonathan read the above quotation in morning meeting for worship and it strongly resonated with Helen. She had been practising meditation and yoga for over 30 years, had received counselling and had come to acknowledge that, although we might experience deep peace during our meditation, and although we might feel changed through the experience (we can call it God, presence), we have to acknowledge that still nothing has changed. Being a body-centred therapist, Helen would say that the body remembers. Our body remembers, even if we don't. It remembers acts of kindness as well as acts of roughness. It remembers when we felt loved and when we felt rejected. As small children, we were unable to reflect on these acts of harshness and rejection. We felt wounded and rejected, which has stayed with us, and we still carry this sense of dislike of self with us.

But we have forgotten that in us is the bubbling presence of life, or God, if you prefer. We can learn to feel this vibrant and joyful energy in ourselves and this will help us to remember that we are loved. In fact, this simple exercise will help us to be present with ourselves; our bodies like to feel the presence of our mind, like a child that can relax when it feels the loving presence of its parent or caregiver.

The musical body practice can help you to relax and is the first step towards loving yourself. It takes about 20–30 minutes. Do it first thing in the morning, or at night before you go to bed. Do it with gentle flowing instrumental music. Choose a piece that you feel really connected to, or maybe try a different one each time. You are invited to sense the music you are listening to in each part of the body, and then in the entire body. Stay with each body part mentioned opposite for about 1 minute (6–8 breaths). Where you have two of a body part (legs, arms, etc.), these are done together.

Start to listen to the music and sense it in your:

feet
ankles
calves
knees
thighs
reproductive organs and sitting bones
hips abdomen chest
shoulders
upper arms
elbows
forearms wrists
hands
shoulder girdle/shoulders
neck
face
head
entire body

When you have completed this practice, having felt the music on a cellular level, stay with the sensations a little longer. If at all possible, just breathe and be. Only when you feel ready, write down mindfully in your journal what you have experienced (this is for your eyes only).

Love (III)

LOVE bade me welcome; yet my soul drew back,
Guilty of dust and sin.
But quick-eyed Love, observing me grow slack
From my first entrance in,
Drew nearer to me, sweetly questioning
If I lack'd anything.

'A guest,' I answer'd, 'worthy to be here:'
Love said, 'You shall be he.'
'I, the unkind, ungrateful? Ah, my dear,
I cannot look on Thee.'
Love took my hand and smiling did reply,
'Who made the eyes but I?'

'Truth, Lord; but I have marr'd them: let my shame
Go where it doth deserve.'
'And know you not,' says Love, 'Who bore
    the blame?'
'My dear, then I will serve.'
'You must sit down,' says Love, 'and taste my meat.'
So I did sit and eat.

George Herbert (1593–1632)

This beautiful poem by George Herbert, made into
a song by the English composer Ralph Vaughan Williams
(1872–1958), may touch some of you deeply; it seems like
a declaration of compassionate love to man. It emphasizes
that the only ingredient we need to bring along for
transforming our self into a living compassion is the
willingness to be present.

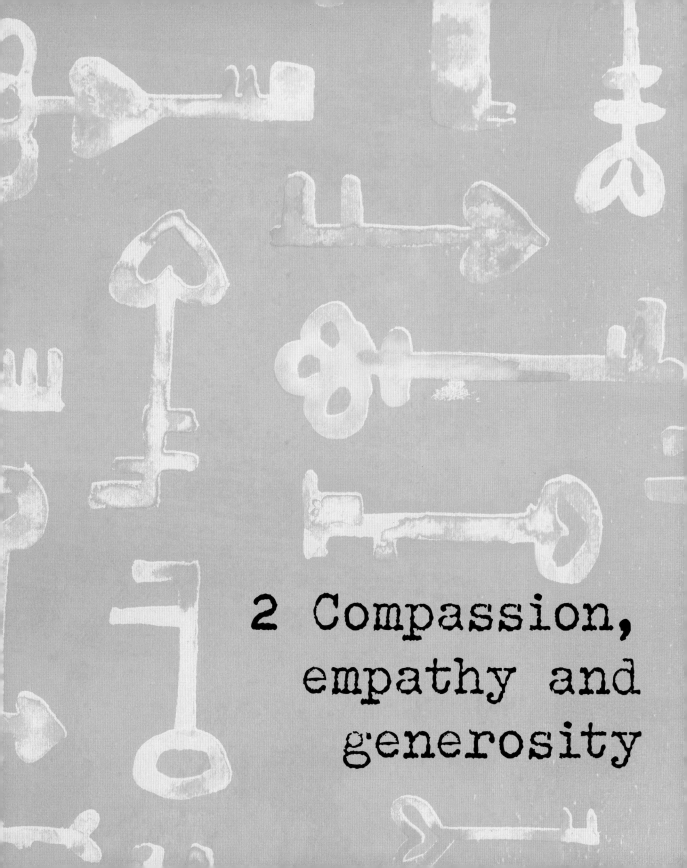

2 Compassion, empathy and generosity

LIFE CAN BE A CHALLENGE. Thousands of years ago, humans lived in small packs of about 30 members. The older, frailer or pregnant ones tended the children, cooked, guarded the camp and nursed the sick, while young and mature males and females went out hunting.

Mammoths, for example, were seen as a great gift (rather like whales are for the Inuit people today). A single specimen could feed the tribe for a long time. The women collected berries and roots on the way, but they also assisted the men during the hunt of wild beasts.

Nowadays, there is much less teamwork, unless you are 'officially' selected to work with others or like to participate in forms of sport that are conducted by one team playing against another. The desire to genuinely offer help to others, without wanting something in return, is seen as unwise. After all, we are living in difficult times and you never know when something may come in handy. So the general trend is to hoard everything. Hoarding has long been recognized as a mental illness. People who hoard feel safer with the things around them than with people. Alongside this, however, are the general hoarders – that is, most of us – who have spare rooms, garages, lofts and sheds full of stuff, either for emergencies or simply because they are too busy to give surplus items away.

Generosity is the desire to aid another simply because you wish to do so. You share your energy, belongings, talents, time and abilities with others instead of keeping everything in store for yourself. You do it without the slightest ulterior motive.

I expect to pass through this world but once; any good thing therefore that I can do, or any kindness that I can show to any fellow creature, let me do it now; let me not defer or neglect it, for I shall not pass this way again.

Widely attributed to the Quaker missionary Stephen Grellet (1773–1855)

Empathy

When we experience distressing moments, just being there for each other is balm for our souls. If you have to go to a court hearing or to hospital for an operation or to receive a diagnosis, a person who cares for you will want to accompany you. The simple act of sharing the experience lessens the load in your heart. Empathic presence is in itself a comforting act. You just sense deep in your awareness that others share the same needs as you. This is called empathy. Empathy has an emotional part and a part that comprehends. It starts with the desire to understand anothers situation without adding to or taking away from it.

At times, you may feel the need to talk something through, even if the other person has no answers; empathic listening can offer healing in itself. This is because just by being with another who truly pays attention you feel that they have entered your world of experiences. Empathic listening can be heart-rending, particularly when you hear about and observe someone elses fears, confusions, anger, despair or even traumas. You are simply there for the other person in need – without judgement. It is a selfless act of kindness to open your heart deeply to the sorrows of another.

Empathy is often transmitted subtly and non-verbally. A simple glance can express that you understand the other's despair, and holding their hand when they receive bad news can be a powerful support.

What is it that helps us to connect so strongly in such a way? Is it a response we learned by observing others when we were young? Empathy is generated by special brain cells referred to as 'mirror neurons'. Researchers in Italy found that we learn to feel empathy by watching and mimicking others. When we see someone engage in a recognizable act, our brain thinks that we are also doing or experiencing it. Scientists are certain that the brain can simulate a physiological action in a psychological form. Neuroscientist Vittorio Gallese, at the University of Parma, says: 'This neural mechanism is involuntary and automatic ... we don't have to think about what other people are doing or feeling, we simply know.'

This phenomenon serves a vital role in relationships. The mirror neurons indicate that there is indeed a true connection between seeing something and then acting accordingly, or experiencing something and feeling the consequences. These brain cells are the feeding ground for empathy. The reason you are so passionate when watching your favourite tennis champion play, and why you want to observe great athletes or actors in order to improve your own performance, and the reason for your ability to relate deeply to other people's situations and emotions are all related to mirror neurons. So, when you exclaim to a friend that you have 'been there' and know how it feels, these are not just empty words. You are indeed feeling their emotions, thanks to your mirror neurons.

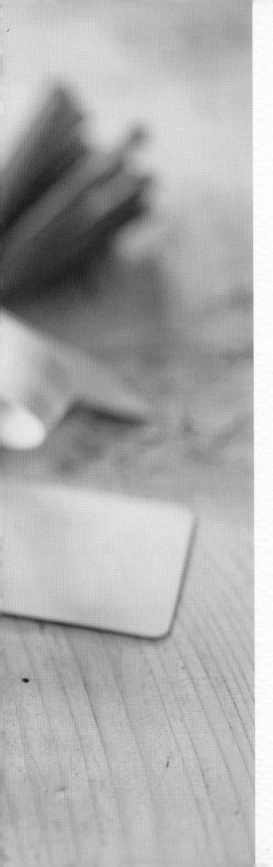

The Power of Love

Through Love bitter things taste sweet.

Through Love pains become as healing balms.

Through Love thorns turn into roses.

Through Love vinegar becomes sweet wine.

Through Love hard stones turn soft like butter.

Through Love soft wax becomes hard iron.

Through Love grief has the flavour of joy.

Through Love stings are like honey.

Through Love lions are harmless as mice.

Through Love sickness is health.

Through Love the dead come to life.

Through Love the king is humble as a slave.

Jalal al-Din Rumi (1207-1273)

Generosity

Once you can truly sense and accept that all beings have needs and know life's struggle, and you want to 'open up' or help them satisfy those needs, you go a step further and enter the domain of generosity. Generosity could be described as the deliberate aspiration to release and diminish the distress and suffering of others.

The intention to benefit somebody else is not dependent on the size of the gift or the gesture you offer, but rather on the pure purpose that comes with it. You are probably familiar with this deeply in your heart. Most of us genuinely admire others who can give without seeking anything in return.

Rick Foster and Greg Hicks wrote a book called *How We Choose to Be Happy* (Putnam, 1999), in which they tell the story of a 12th-century Spanish philosopher called Maimonides. He apparently wrote about 'real giving from the heart', suggesting that an act of true generosity is to offer a starting place and even work for the needy, so that they can learn to look after themselves and eventually have a chance of independence. In many ways, this is what charities want to achieve nowadays: show people how to build a well and they will learn to do it by themselves.

How does generosity lead to well-being? Even children know intuitively how to share and offer the gift of a 'hug', a smile, a flower, a drawing or something else they have made. It feels simply good to give, sometimes better than to receive.

Research at institutions such as the Institute of Cognitive Science, France; Harvard University, USA; and the University of Amsterdam, the Netherlands, suggests that generosity leads to a higher release of the hormone oxytocin. Also released by breast-feeding mothers, oxytocin reduces blood pressure and levels of the stress hormone cortisol, increases pain thresholds, diminishes fear, and stimulates a variety of positive social interactions. It also evokes feelings of satisfaction and reduces anxiety. Cortisol recedes when we are less anxious, which means that our brain's faculties are able to work more efficiently. Many studies, such as those carried out at Rosock and Justus-Liebig Universities in Germany and at the University of Zurich, Switzerland, have shown a correlation of oxytocin with deepening human bonding and trust. Generosity connects us to others, and social connections are a powerful way to increase our own gladness.

People and their generosity

Paul J. Zak, a neuroeconomist at Claremont Graduate University, USA, developed an experiment that looked at people and their generosity. Oxytocin had already been shown to cause trust towards others, so Zak wondered whether it would also make people more generous. Participants were randomly given an amount of money (around $40) and then asked to share it all with other participants. Whether they did or not was up to them – they could, if they wanted, take some of it home. They were not allowed to know what the others were doing, so had to make their own decision. By means of a nasal spray, half the participants were given oxytocin, and the other half salt water. Generosity increased by 80 per cent in the oxytocin group compared to the other group. As participants were leaving the experiment, Zak asked them to donate some of their leftover money to charity. One-third of the participants did so, averaging a $6 donation. Who donated most generously? Those who had already been more generous from the start. Maybe some people just produce more oxytocin and are consequently more generous. Maybe giving and connecting produces more oxytocin, which would make it a potent way to increase one's own gladness.

Generosity can be viewed as a way to show that you care for the well-being of others (loving kindness). You can give your time, share useful contacts, provide a listening ear, mentor somebody, let somebody who expresses a sense of urgency 'jump the queue' (see Sue's story, page 78) or let others get off the train before you do. What touches us deeply is the love, kindness and compassion behind the gesture, however big or small.

This does not necessarily include offering money and getting an official reward by receiving tax reductions or recognition in the news or on television. Of course, it is better to give than do nothing at all, but the sweet point in your heart is only touched when it is the heart alone that knows about the loving deed. In contrast, when we hold back or 'store things', we tend to 'contract' more and fear losing possessions or positions. Too much attachment to things can cause us to suffer more than never having had them in the first place.

Let us look briefly at the notion of 'attachment' from the philosophical view of Buddhism: non-attachment is perhaps the most important learning point of the whole construct. The Dalai Lama once said: 'Attachment is the origin, the root of suffering; hence it is the cause of suffering.'

When you want to practise non-attachment, you are swimming against the stream of society. We are taught from an early age to be better than others and to gain wealth, possessions and power. Young children are still free of these attachments, but when they enter school they begin to learn how to 'exclude' themselves from

others and be more successful than them. We 'desire' more and dislike those who have it. We are all 'invited' to become intrinsically selfish. Rarely are we taught that 'we, we' could be a much easier path through life than 'me, me' – but then we would not be special, more successful and therefore more lovable than others.

Bringing understanding to these facts may help us to let go (at least in part) of this destructive life-path. By understanding that we are all to some degree playing the same 'game', we learn that only by compassion and forgiveness can we start to reduce this self-induced suffering. This does not mean we cannot enjoy a beautiful sunset, a lovely meal or falling in love. Life can be beautiful, but as soon as we absolutely want and must have all these lovely things continuously, we destroy them. The fear of losing them creates 'suffering'. So, living in this moment as well as we can, and being aware that it will pass sooner or later, is probably the best we can do – experiencing, letting go, and being aware of it.

If what you share brings a smile to somebody else's face, you can remember 'the smile' and bring it home to your own body! Even if you sometimes feel you have nothing to give or share, you may forget that a friendly word or a companionable silence is just the action that can take you out of your own sadness and loneliness. Through sharing, you may even discover your own wealth and value.

Generosity can help you relate to belongings in a more resourceful way. Do you make good use of them or could somebody else benefit from them more at this moment? You could help create more abundance all around if you learned to allow objects and energy to move on. Furthermore, you might want to let go a bit of self-interested fixations with 'me'. If giving feels good, it makes sense that extending your capacity to give can make you feel even better.

When I lived in China, I had a friend who was always very generous. I really admired her for this. One day she wore some beautiful blue topaz earrings. I told her how well they suited her and how they complemented her blue eyes. When I attended my leaving party, more than a year later, before returning to the UK, she presented me with a little box. When I opened it, I could hardly believe it – she had given me her beautiful earrings. I was taken aback and at first did not want to accept them, but she insisted, saying: 'They will look even better on you.' She showed me how beautiful true generosity feels, and I always think of her when I wear them.

Generosity is a potent way of growing and maturing in compassion.

Ute Bock

A person who has devoted her life to the needy is Ute Bock. She is one of the 'PeaceWomen across the Globe' (see www.1000peacewomen.org) and lives in Vienna, Austria, where she helps refugees. Her motto is: 'It is not wise to establish a group of underprivileged people. Even if these people can, or are forced to, move back to their homeland, it is better that they learn something here.'

Ute worked as a social worker and teacher until her retirement in 2000. She had started to take care of teenage immigrants in the 1970s. While initially these were children of immigrant workers, she later began to accommodate teenage refugees from war-torn countries. She never sent a youth away, no matter where they came from. When she could no longer put them up herself, she began to hire and finance flat-sharing apartments for them to live communally.

Since retiring, she has spent most of her time developing a community of 50 apartments, housing more than 200 African immigrants, and has become known as 'Mama Africa'.

Ute used her own pension, her savings, financial awards and donations to finance her project. Some call her the 'Grande Dame of the Outcasts', while many consider her to be weird for spending her time and money as she does. I like this kind of weirdness: Ute does not expect anything in return and feels joyful about what she does.

We should give as we would receive, cheerfully, quickly, and without hesitation; for there is no grace in a benefit that sticks to the fingers.

Seneca (c. 4 BC–AD 65)

Practice: Generosity 'challenge'

Try thinking creatively how you could give more to others than you usually do in terms of time, skills and resources – are you willing to go beyond your comfort zone? Maybe commit to a little gesture now.

1   In your journal, write down one kind or generous thing you could do every day for a week. Before starting, check your mood on a scale of 1 (very low) to 10 (very high). What is your present mood state? When you have done one generous deed a day, assess how you are feeling. Try to be honest and realistic. Also notice how others respond to you when you are practising kindness.

2   Sit down and remember someone who has impressed you with their generosity; you might think of a personal friend, a famous person or even a character from a story, play or film. Suddenly *A Christmas Carol* by Charles Dickens' comes to mind: Scrooge is transformed by becoming generous. If you like, write down the names of people you know or remember who are open-handed and open-hearted, recalling what kind of deeds they engage in.

3   Write down a list of things and actions you can freely offer without hesitation, even to strangers. Then try to do at least one thing every day or week (choose your own timing) and write down afterwards how it felt in your body, what thoughts came up and whether you might try it again.

Practice: **Developing generosity**

1 Sit comfortably, wearing a scarf around your shoulders to avoid feeling cold, and settle into your awareness by grounding your feet and focusing on your breath for a while. Let go of thoughts, images, feelings and sounds, and enjoy the experience of coming to rest in stillness.

2 Focus on internally visualizing yourself being present in your favourite room. Take a look around and pass your gaze over all the objects it contains. Remember how you received many of them as gifts. Maybe even remember the place where you received some of them and the person(s) who gave them to you.

3 Can you take your mind back to the moment you received one or several of the gifts, the expression on the person's face when they handed it to you, and the feeling you had at the time? Each occasion will carry its own memory. Maybe you even gave a gift to yourself. Where did it come from? What is it made of? Who may have been part of the process of creating the gift in the first place? Stretch your mind as far as possible, to encompass everyone who helped to bring you this gift.

4 Consider the idea that it is only through the kindness of others that you enjoy possessions, sustenance and nurture. In fact, we all work together to keep each other alive and well.

5 Finish this meditation by bringing to mind some of the generous gift-bearers, and offer them kindness by using the words: 'May you all be safe and protected, may you all be joyful, peaceful and adventurous, and may you all live with ease and with generosity.'

When your heart continues bleeding

He had eyes that seemed much too far apart, they sat deeply in their sockets and were dark. His eyes were not peaceful, uncountable tiny wrinkles covered his face, his skin was brown and leathery – like the skin of a farmer who works high up in the mountains.

Many hours of sunshine and rough weather and tears had left their etchings behind. There were many scars on his left hand. He was bony and his shoulders hung down in a tired kind of way. He smelled of alcohol and air. His odour somehow belonged to his eyes. These sad eyes, which had lost so very much … He grabbed the guitar. He only knew two chords: C and C7. He used these to accompany himself when he sang. He had no strength to add to those songs, but never-ending passion. There was also a very distinct manner to his performance, which let you sense his broken heart.

I got up and danced to a French ballade. His crying voice, which nevertheless filled the room, smelled like a strong and heavy dark wine from the country.

A while later we both sat at a wooden table on the outside terrace of the hostel. We looked into one another's eyes for a long silence and I played the guitar a little.

Then he started to tell his story in French. I understood that he had lost his wife, both of his sons and parents in a road accident a couple of years ago. Also last year his only brother and his family crashed and died.

Within one year losing everybody who matters, all who were born from the same blood … he wanted to end his life – scars on his hand. But instead of dying he went all the way to Santiago de Compostela and back. His heart was still bleeding after he returned. Emptiness, so much emptiness! Surely God must know why and what for? So much suffering, so many tears. No money.

In the evening he once again sat outside the church begging. He loves God. He is once again on the journey to Santiago. He never wants to return to France. He is only 44 years old, yet looks like 60. He talks a lot, almost two hours go by. I cannot understand much at all, but my eyes are listening with attention. I like him. Deep and yet endearing sadness lies between us. He asks whether he can shoot a photo of me. I sing 'The Sound of Silence' and smile at him.

In the evening I see him one more time. I give him all of my delicious Tyrolean smoked bacon and a little money for a few swigs to forget for a little while. A last glimpse, the first and last embrace.

'A meeting on the way to Santiago de Compostela' by Lisa Kutmon (translated by Patrizia Collard)

3 Me, me, me and being good enough

The Narcissism Epidemic covers a broad range of cultural symptoms, including increases in materialism, entitlement, public violence and aggression, self-promotion, and the desire for uniqueness.

From *The Narcissm Epidemic* **Jean M. Twenge and W. Keith Campbell**

A NEW EPIDEMIC IS SWIFTLY infecting more and more individuals. Loving yourself too much leads eventually to thinking you may, indeed, be the 'centre of the universe'.

When researching their book *The Narcissm Epidemic* (Free Press, Simon and Schuster, 2009) American psychologists Jean M. Twenge and W. Keith Campbell found that about 80 per cent of students think they are well above average, more than 90 per cent of university lecturers think they teach better than their colleagues, and a similar number of drivers believe they are more skilled than others who use the road.

Twenge says: 'What's really become prevalent over the last two decades is the idea that being highly self-confident – loving yourself, believing in yourself – is the key to success. Now the interesting thing about that belief is it's widely held, it's very deeply held, and it's also untrue.' In psychology, this tendency is called Narcissism.

Keeping your feet on the ground

In Greek mythology, Narcissus was a young man who fell in love with his own image when he saw a reflection of himself in a pool of water. The disorder is not necessarily obvious at first sight. The narcissist appears energetic, has high self-confidence, is eloquent and charming, and has better skills (logic, knowledge, wisdom, intelligence, objectivity) than most of his peers, yet emotionally he appears distant. He basically lacks empathy and compassion for others, and is driven to the top of his chosen goal, never mind who might get in his way. To him, being average is like having a disease, the worst you can have.

If you follow people in their teens, twenties and thirties on the internet, you will notice that they constantly put new photos of themselves on their social networking site. They count how many 'tweets' or messages they have received each day, or even each hour, and how many 'friends' and 'followers' they have. This, however, leads us to the sad fact that those who are left out or receive only a few messages often feel so low that they may become depressed, self-harm or commit suicide.

Even the youngest children are reared with the belief that they are more than special; you can buy baby T-shirts with messages such as 'I love myself' and 'I + I', which encourage a certain type of behaviour from the start.

Every day we can experience famous people sharing their daily life on TV reality shows or talk shows. We have an obsession with physical beauty, which often leads to surgical procedures in order to achieve the perfect look. All of this increases exhibitionism and focusing on 'me and me alone'. What falls by the wayside is an open-minded ability to self-reflect and genuinely care for anybody but oneself.

Sooner or later, however, the inflated ego causes others to retreat and reject the narcissus. Partners and friends need emotional connection, empathy, kindness and gratitude. If they regularly miss out on these responses, they will leave, and suddenly the self-obsessed high-flyer is all alone – really, really alone. This often leads to depression and suicide as a final act of revenge. When a narcissist accesses psychotherapy, he still hopes that the therapist will change the world for him. Narcissists are among the most complicated clients.

It is extremely difficult and takes a long time to treat this disorder successfully. Meditations focusing on the breath and on 'grounding oneself' have shown good results in helping sufferers to reconnect to their whole self. Thereafter, it is necessary to teach them how to show compassion and kindness towards others by, for example, asking their partner how they are and what they experienced today, or by holding and cuddling their children when they are anxious and sad.

Case study 1

I once treated a young lady who was deeply steeped in narcissistic self-obsession. She was generally feeling physically cold and needing a blanket and a hot drink. There were many tears about her boyfriend, who just did not understand that she simply could not wash her hair herself and that only hairdressers could do this job properly. It was not that he minded her spending the money, but the fact was that all of the daily activities, even on Saturday, revolved around her hairdresser appointments. It was not just the boyfriend who was troublesome to her either, but also her girlfriends, who simply did not understand when she refused to go away for a weekend or would only go to spas that had a hairdresser on site.

I tried. I really put all my compassion into the work with her, because she was truly suffering. On several occasions she cancelled therapy appointments at relatively short notice, but I only charge clients if cancellations occur less than 24 hours prior to the arranged time and are not health-related. So, when such a cancellation once again occurred (a business meeting – she was a very well-paid solicitor), I reminded her of the policy and said that this time I would have to charge her. Then an avalanche of verbal abuse came my way, and she neither paid nor made another appointment. I was her sixth therapist in two years. I rest my case.

Case study 2

An encounter with a male client had interesting challenges. He was a stunning-looking man and highly intelligent. He had fathered a child in his previous relationship (but was no longer in touch with the child), and had two more in his present one. He just could not understand why all women were so demanding. He said he was there and helped sometimes but, really, wasn't he supposed to earn the living? Similarly, his clients were all totally unrealistic, expecting him, an interior designer, to get all the work done overnight. He said that they should be glad that he even bothered with such boring little projects.

Soon he had a mission to sort out his therapist's interior design problems, too; when I gently reminded him that this was not an option while we were working together and, furthermore, that I quite liked my style, he huffed and puffed and laughed about my narrow-mindedness and taking all these rules as written in stone. 'Come on,' he said, 'you know nobody sticks to rules any more.' He suggested that I was really childish.

Thereafter, he tested my boundaries even further and did not turn up for an appointment, but apologized. I said that this time I would not charge him, but if it happened again, I would. Sooner rather than later, he failed to turn up for a scheduled appointment, so I wrote to him and explained that I expected him to settle accounts if he wanted me to continue working with him. He slipped into the 'nasty child' role and said that nobody could tell him what to do, and that hairdressers also lost their income when clients did not turn up. I just repeated that I would not continue seeing him unless this issue was resolved. He promised (begrudgingly) to put the money in an envelope, and guess what … it never happened. This was particularly astonishing since he was also self-employed and had been complaining bitterly when clients took too long to settle their accounts.

Getting the balance right

Even if we do not belong to the 'elite of narcissists', there is another way to feel superior to our fellow humans. All we need to do is to see others as inferior to ourselves. We talk about others behind their back, looking for their flaws and our strengths. It is a favourite pastime of many to buy magazines such as *Hello* and see stars or celebrities looking chubby in their bikinis, having a 'bad hair day' or coming out of a club looking intoxicated or exhausted. We find a certain pleasure in seeing others at their worst, and that feeds into negative thinking patterns and separation from others.

The nature of a dualistic universe regularly shows, however, that although some of us often feel 'better' or 'satisfied' in an unhealthy way by putting others down, we have an equally destructive habit of criticizing ourselves and permanently feeling not good enough. What happens to individuals who are *not* high-flyers, beautiful and intelligent, or rich or important? Many feel rather desolate, thinking they are not good enough, for it seems that striving for perfection is more and more the normal thing to do. So, for those who are not part of the 'inner circle' of the rich, successful and beautiful, however much they desire to be part of it, life is constantly challenging, particularly because the worst critic lives inside your mind. The author and psychologist Kristin Neff says: 'The language of self-criticism cuts like a knife.'

I would like to introduce you briefly to a form of counselling called Transactional Analysis (TA) that endeavours to help individuals find their own balance, their own unique signature in life. It is an approach that teaches you to see the special light that you may bring to the world, autonomously and spontaneously.

I find TA extremely useful for compassionate self-awareness and insight. It focuses on three 'states of being', or roles, that are an inherent part of every individual.

All of us move between the roles of parent, adult and child. The parent role creates and implements regulations, many of which you may have picked up from significant adults in your formative years. The adult is the rational decision-maker, and the child acts out your sensory and emotional side.

Each aspect once again reflects the universal dualism mentioned earlier. The parent can be nurturing or critical; the child can be spontaneous, but also self-centred and irresponsible. As always in life, equanimity and balance will help you to experience life more harmoniously, and it is the adult's job to encourage these.

Problems occur when you are stuck too long in any of these 'ego states'. Here are some examples. If you are constantly telling yourself off, never thinking you are good enough, pushing yourself so hard that you can barely cope any more, you may be stuck in the state of the 'critical parent'. If, on the other hand, you always want to have everything you fancy, for however long you desire it, and sulk or explode if you hear even a gentle 'no more', you may be trapped in the 'spoilt inner child' state. Last, but not least, if you are genuinely so balanced that you may be perceived as dull or boring, then the adult has the upper hand too often.

Of course, it would be most helpful if you could compassionately observe your life and transfer some of the above ideas onto patterns that you know do not serve you. But you need to have compassion with all the parts that make up the whole of you. The kind and benevolent parent supervises and protects, but does not extinguish the flame, the adult cares and supports your actions, and the child is wild, free and creative.

Wherever you go,
go with all your heart.

Confucius (551–479BC)

Practice: Getting unstuck and recycling

1   In your journal, create three columns with the headings 'Parent', 'Child' and 'Adult'.

2   Fill in under each heading your typical behaviour and thought patterns – the ones that serve you well and the ones that get in the way or cause you pain.

3   Choose two colours: one for the aspects you want to keep, and the other for those you want to discard.

4   Circle kindly and helpful patterns with the 'keep' colour, and trapping and painful ones with the 'discard' colour.

5   Last, but not least, imagine you are a detective and observe yourself acting in real life. Whenever you find yourself slipping into a 'discard' behaviour pattern, consider how you can replace the action or thought with a more helpful one. Use a third colour for the new action.

People should think less about what they ought to do and more about what they ought to be.

Meister Eckhart, mystic (1260–1328)

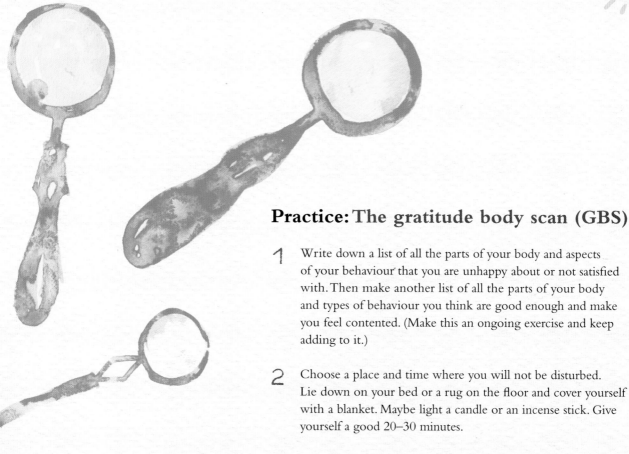

Practice: The gratitude body scan (GBS)

1   Write down a list of all the parts of your body and aspects of your behaviour that you are unhappy about or not satisfied with. Then make another list of all the parts of your body and types of behaviour you think are good enough and make you feel contented. (Make this an ongoing exercise and keep adding to it.)

2   Choose a place and time where you will not be disturbed. Lie down on your bed or a rug on the floor and cover yourself with a blanket. Maybe light a candle or an incense stick. Give yourself a good 20–30 minutes.

3   Start with your feet and slowly and mindfully work all the way up to your torso, finishing with the head. When you start with a body part, focus on sensing it and then give thanks for how it has served you well. Don't differentiate between the so-called 'pretty' ones and those you would rather change. Thank each part for what it has enabled you to do. For example, thank your feet for making it possible for you to walk. Also add to the GBS the good actions you could perform because of the functionality of the different parts of your body. So, with your hands, for example, linger a little while just sensing them and then add: 'Thank you, hands, for helping me to bake cookies, which give joy to my friends and neighbours.'

Every GBS will be a little different. As best you can, allow each practice to unfold moment by moment; the more you notice how well parts of your being have assisted you, the less likely you are to focus purely on their physical appearance.

Daisy Notgoodenough

There once was a kind lady called Daisy who was extremely keen to help others. She got up in the morning before sunrise and had a shower. While having the shower, she made lists in her head, such as what she had to do for her friends and neighbours, who to call in order to find out whether they needed any help, or which TV programmes to watch so she could see who suffered and decide who needed her practical or financial support next.

She was a busy lady, as you may have guessed, but she got a lot of pleasure out of helping others. After all, she pondered, so many people are selfish and greedy and just live a life without purpose. I would hate such a life, she often thought to herself.

Every day she looked in the mirror and smiled. She said to herself: 'Ah well, I will never win a beauty pageant: my eyes are too small, my lips too thin, my nose too big, my hair too mousy, my legs too short and my feet too big. But who needs a prize if you can make others happy?

One day she got up at 5 am as usual and had her daily shower. This is strange, she thought, it is freezing cold – both the water and the radiator. But soon she was caught up in her list-making and finished her cold shower in no time. When she tried to make her cup of tea, she noticed that the electricity was not working either. She thought: 'Oh well, I will put a pan on the gas stove and will make porridge and tea this way.'

So she got out of the house before 6 am and started her usual round of chosen duties. She brought a meal to a homeless man who camped in the park. She went to Mrs Smith, a 93-year-old bedridden lady, got her washed and dressed, made her breakfast and even read a poem to her. Then she went to church to clean the chairs and the floor and water the flowers, and so on … and it was dark and past 6 pm before she got home. She noticed again that her flat felt really cold, but she thought it was too late to ring anybody for help. Even the TV did not work, so she just had a sandwich and went to bed feeling very tired, as usual.

For three days and nights she was without heating. On the fourth day, she woke up feeling very hot and thought: 'Thank God, the heating is back on.' Alas, she was wrong. She had caught a very bad cold. She was getting more and more poorly, but continued doing her duties. Eventually, on the fifth morning, she decided to call her neighbour as she could barely get out of bed. When Mrs Cross rang the doorbell and Daisy opened the door, Mrs Cross gasped at the sight of her. 'Daisy,' she said, 'what have you done to yourself? Oh dear, oh dear.'

Daisy does not remember much after that, but suddenly, or so it seemed, she woke up in a hospital bed and was very worried. She thought 'Who will feed the man in the park, who will help Mrs Smith, who will water the flowers?', and so on.

Dr Allright came to see her. Daisy was shocked to hear that she had a very bad chest infection and was not allowed to get back to her round of duties for at least a week. She cried in desperation. Dr Allright said: 'Daisy, I do not usually give people advice. I usually just administer help and medicine. But this time I will make an exception. Mrs Cross told me about you and your kindness and how it seemingly has driven you near to self-destruction. We have found five volunteers who are looking after your duties so you can recover and feel at peace. But being too good could have cost you your life, and who would have benefited from that? Nobody, least of all you.'

Daisy just muttered: 'I don't care much about myself. I will never be noticed for my beauty: my eyes are too small, my lips too thin, my nose too big, my hair too mousy, my legs too short and my feet too big. So, I thought to myself, I need to be kind, for at least that will be something to be happy about.'

Dr Allright said: 'Listen to me, Daisy.' He looked really stern and serious. 'Unless you start being good to yourself right now, you will no longer be able to be kind to others.' Then he smiled and squeezed her hand and Daisy smiled and squeezed him back. He said: 'You have a beautiful smile, and a beautiful heart. I think you are the loveliest lady I have met for a long time.'

Here is a short story that might connect to the curiosity of your inner child. This is the part of you that may be most open to change and insight.

Practice: The inner critic, the sufferer and the compassionate observer

Adapted and developed from *Self-Compassion (stop beating yourself up and leave insecurity behind)* by Kristin Neff, PhD (Hodder and Stoughton, 2011).

1   Set up three chairs in a circle. If it is helpful, put cushions or something else on the chair you are not sitting on so that they look occupied.

2   Think of one aspect of your behaviour, ability or look for which you often criticize yourself.

3   Visualize your inner critic sitting on one chair (they could look slightly like you, only harsher and meaner; alternatively, if you had a critical adult in your formative years, it could be them). Then imagine, in the second chair, your heart centre – the compassionate observer (it could take the form of a person who loves you unconditionally or a kindly human or spirit that wishes you well). Sit down on the third chair. You are the injured party, the one who suffers.

4   Now think of a recent problem that you found difficult to let go of. For example, your presentation at work did not go well, you think, because nobody stayed behind to ask any questions, and neither did anybody congratulate you.

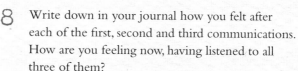

8   Write down in your journal how you felt after
each of the first, second and third communications.
How are you feeling now, having listened to all
three of them?

7   This time it is your turn: tell the inner critic
how hurt you feel and try to engage in what the
compassionate observer suggested to you: 'I really
don't like you always just looking at the bad or
"not good enough" stuff. I don't want you to hurt
me or criticize me any longer. I don't need to listen
to you. Your words are not altogether true; I really
think that. I feel quite pleased that I managed to
get through the whole speech without stuttering.
I think I projected my voice well. I even managed
to tell a joke and maybe they just left because they
wanted to catch the last train home. They have to
come back to work tomorrow morning. Let's see
what feedback I may get then.'

6   Then listen to the compassionate observer: 'Hey,
did you forget how the lady in the front row really
laughed for minutes when you told the joke?
Remember how they applauded you at the end.
You really did your best. I am proud of you.
Also, can you think of any other reason why the
audience left swiftly after your talk? Just try, and if
you can't think of one I will help you out. OK?'

5   Listen to what the inner critic has to say: 'Well, of
course, you little lousy presenter, you were boring,
boring, boring; you can call yourself lucky that at
least some of them showed up.'

The Roots of Tears

Let your soul lend its ear to every cry of pain.
As a lotus bears its heart to drink the morning sun.
Let not the fierce sun dry one tear of pain before
You yourself have wiped it from the sufferer's eye.
But let each burning human tear fall on your heart!
And there remain, nor even brush it off
Until the pain that caused it is removed.

Vedic meditation

Compassion is a verb.

Thich Nhat Hanh, Buddhist monk (1926–)

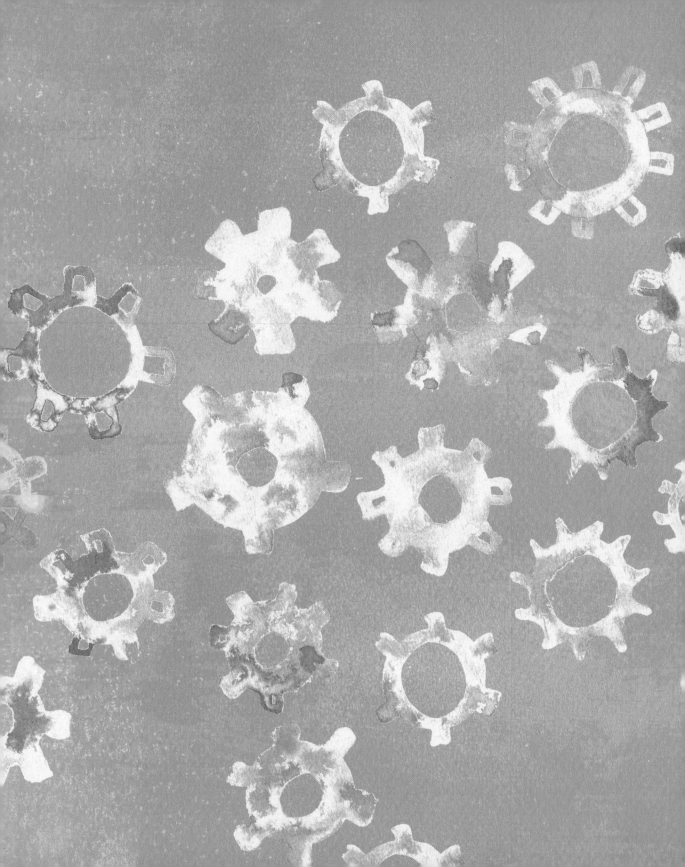

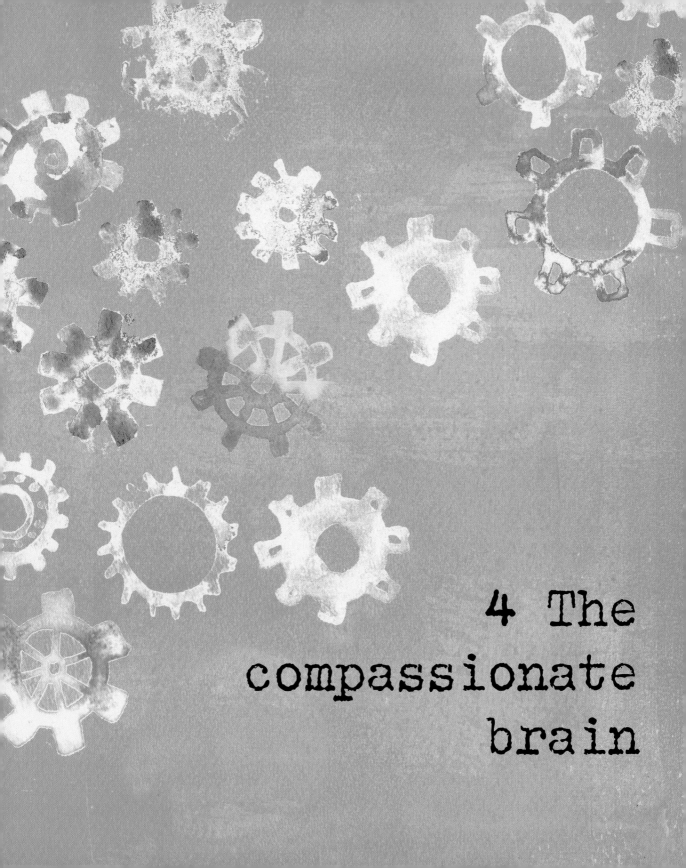

4 The compassionate brain

PAUL GILBERT, AN EMINENT RESEARCHER and teacher of
compassion, says that Mother Nature was keen to equip
us with a brain that could react very quickly to threat
and even remember or foresee dangerous situations. Thus
our species survived. But Mother Nature was not really
interested in whether we were having a good time while
surviving. Having such a quickly aroused 'fight or flight'
response does not help us to live calmly and joyfully.

Around thirty years ago, most neuroscientists were
convinced that adult brains were 'finished' products that
would only change for the worse through ageing or
strokes, but this view is now completely outdated. Today
we know that, due to its neuroplasticity, it is possible for
the brain to continue evolving as long as it is stimulated
and used. For example, a study by Elizabeth Hellmuth
Margulis at Northwestern Univesity, USA, using magnetic
resonance imaging (MRI) scans of violinists who practised
several hours a day, showed that the areas of the brain
controlling their finger movements grew larger.

Margolis noted that: 'There are lots of studies
showing that musicians' brains have different
networks than those of people who haven't had
formal musical training.'

In another experiment, violinists and flautists listened
to music played on the violin and the flute while in
an MRI scanner. Margolis found that violinists' brains,
when they listen to violin music, look like flutists'
brains when they listen to flute music. Their intensive
input had created their special network.

Can the brain change?

In 1994, the neuroscientist Professor Richard Davidson joined the Mind and Life Institute (see page 75), and he and his team set out to explore aspects of the neuroplastic brain. He was interested to find out what happened to a brain (such as that of a Tibetan monk) if it was exposed to thousands of hours of meditation, and hypothesized that meditation practice triggered plastic changes in the brain. Would such a brain only change temporarily when responding to meditative inputs or triggers, or might it even change structurally? It was a long time before he could start this research properly.

In 2001, His Holiness the 14th Dalai Lama visited Davidson in his laboratory. His Holiness offered him help and was seemingly fascinated by the idea of observing 'scientifically' what practitioners of Buddhist meditations had known through their personal experience for at least two and a half thousand years. Meditation changes you; how you think, how you behave and, most of all, how you feel. Until Davidson's ground-breaking research, 'Buddhist and Psychological Perspectives on Emotions and Well-Being', reported in *Current Directions in Psychological Science* in 2005, we only knew from observation that regular practice of mindful or compassion meditation changes your reactions to threat: you become calmer, respond more wisely, and return to a state of equilibrium more quickly.

Davidson was seen as an idealist for wanting to prove not only that mind-states such as gladness, empathy and enthusiasm could be trained, but also that these skills would change your brain significantly for as long as you practised regularly – even, if you chose, until the end of your days. His goal was to promote insight into the possibility that the aforementioned practices could not only cure mental imbalance but also improve anybody's mental and emotional health.

Just as brushing your teeth, eating your recommended five portions of fruit and vegetables and regular exercise are nowadays accepted means of maintaining and improving physical health, these meditative practices might one day be prescribed as a daily life skill for remaining mentally robust and well. In 2005, Davidson and his colleagues wanted to invest preventative and positive interventions for people who had not yet developed any signs of mental illness. They wanted to promote staying well, not only getting well.

How compassion meditation affects the brain

One of Professor Davidson's earlier experiments at the University of Wisconsin-Madison was carried out with non-meditators. He explained to some of them that when they saw an 'image of suffering' they should focus on compassion: 'Have an aspiration that this person may become well, happy and free of suffering.' While these ordinary people were being monitored in a functional magnetic resonance imaging (fMRI) scanner, they were shown a photograph of a child with an enormous tumour growing out of his eye. Those who had been given no prior explanation had an emotional response of repulsion and a strong signal of activation of the amygdala (this is the 'control centre' in the brain that responds to destructive emotions such as suffering, panic, irritation and worry, and activates the stress response). However, those participants who had been asked to be compassionate (it was only an aspiration with no training in compassion) had a reduced signal in their amygdala. So modulation could be achieved with mental training, and the more training you had, the more change was to be expected.

Matthieu Ricard has a PhD in cellular genetics and left France to study Buddhism in the Himalayas and Nepal more than 40 years ago. He often acts as the French translator for the Dalai Lama and, as a trained scientist, was very keen to get involved in Davidson's experiments.

The experiments started with electroencephalography (EEG), a technique that measures electrical activity in the brain through tiny electrodes placed on the scalp.

Tibetan monks have clean-shaven heads – so there were few problems attaching the 256 electrodes to Ricard's scalp. Ricard and seven other monks and a control group, consisting of eight people who did not regularly meditate but had received a one-week introductory course in compassion meditation, were observed while meditating with the intention of 'unlimited compassion' towards all beings. Thus they would focus not on a specific person and their suffering but on humanity at large, which as a concept is much more abstract. The participants were instructed to switch between meditating and non-meditating.

When Davidson analysed the collected data, he found that a strong enhancement of gamma waves had occurred during the compassion meditation. The readings reflected activation of mental effort and the fact that remote brain circuits were being connected (in layman's terms, these bring together different aspects of sensory awareness – look, touch, sound, smell, etc. – to help the brain identify an object, such as an apple or a cat).

When Ricard started to meditate, his gamma waves immediately got stronger, but even when he stopped the meditation (and also during the switching periods) they did not reduce. The increase in his gamma-wave activity was greater than any other measurement that had ever been reported. The other monks also had huge increases, lasting five minutes rather than the expected milliseconds. The monks' brains were different –

the changes were enduring brain qualities that created a lasting compassionate state. Davidson found that the longer and more frequently a monk had meditated – some had been on three-year silent retreats, for example, and had meditated for more than 50,000 hours – the more significant the brain changes were. It was also interesting that those in the control group had slight but meaningful increases in gamma waves, which was unexpected because they had only received a small amount of training in compassion meditation.

Ricard then offered to participate in another experiment using an MRI scanner. Once again, he was to switch on the compassion practice and then go into a neutral state, alternating several times. The other participants followed suit. One extra element was introduced – from time to time they heard a scream. When meditating on compassion, there was a more significant response to listening to the scream than when not meditating. Was this proof that compassionate mind-states responded more deeply to the suffering of another?

The brains of the monks showed higher activation in several regions. One of them was the anterior cingulate cortex (ACC), which is responsible for cognition and related functions, as well as for decision-making, empathy and regulating emotions. Furthermore, their brains showed more activity in the regions used for planned movement. Were they perhaps ready to go

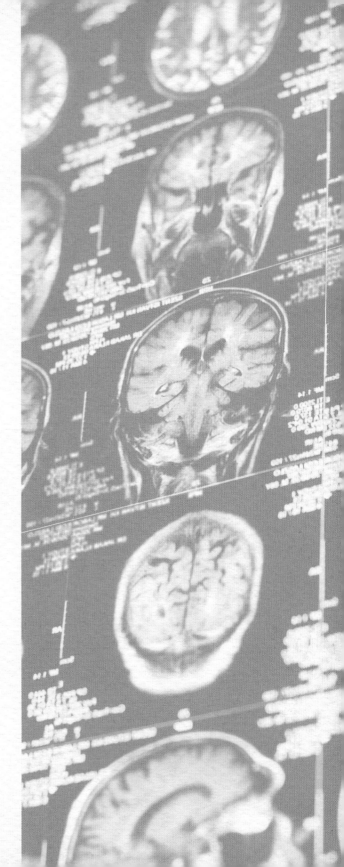

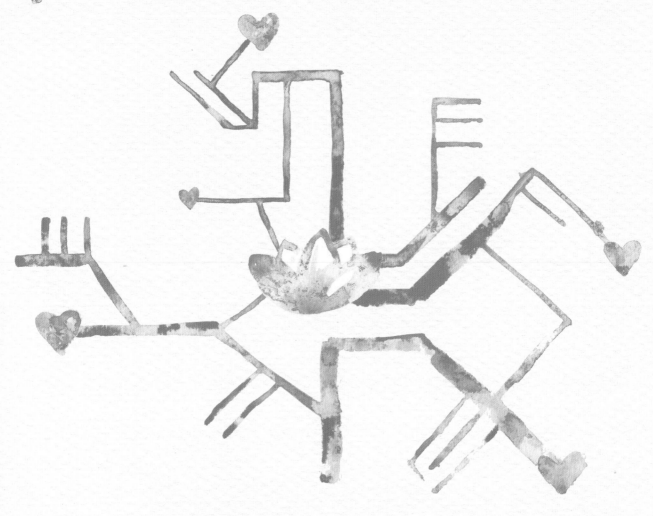

and help the unknown people who were suffering? Davidson described these findings to the Dalai Lama, and they are recorded by the science writer Sharon Begley in her book *The Plastic Mind*, (Ballantine Books, 2007): 'They seem to have a disposition to act in the face of suffering ... they are moved by compassion.' Ricard adds: 'It is a state of complete benevolence, of complete readiness, with no limitations.'

Lastly, one other area was activated, and it makes me smile when writing this: the part of the prefrontal cortex (PFC) associated with happiness lit up. Ricard has been called 'the happiest man on Earth' because he also has an amygdala that has shrunk from the size of an almond to that of a raisin. He can remain still when a loud noise (such as a door slamming or a gunshot) occurs near him. He does smile most of the time, as do the Dalai

Lama and the other monks … and their smiles seem genuine. Having been very near to both Ricard and the Dalai Lama at two different events, I can honestly say that I *felt* their smiles.

Richard Davidson tells in an interview with neuropsychologist Rick Hanson that when he accompanied the Dalai Lama through a hospital corridor where many sick people stood or sat in their wheelchairs, the Dalai Lama stopped in front of every person and smiled at them. A walk that should have taken five minutes took 45. But such is the strength of compassion that the energy in the corridor was vibrating with kindness – it literally is a felt experience.

In summary, compassion meditation does 'generate affection, empathy and the desire to help others. This clearly indicates meditation changes the function of the brain in an enduring way.' Davidson continues: 'As a neuroscientist, I have to believe that engaging in compassion meditation every day for an hour … would change your brain in important ways.' So he recommends starting – even if just for a few minutes – having compassion for yourself or somebody you love, or even a pet. Plant that seed and water it regularly. There was definite change in the control group described above, who had practised for only one week.

We are not fixed. Change is possible, brains are adaptable and we can and must cultivate the attitude of compassion towards others.

The Mind and Life Institute

The Mind and Life Institute is a charitable institution that aims to study the human mind and the benefits of meditative practices. It investigates both experiential knowing from the world's contemplative traditions and findings from contemporary scientific research. Ultimately, its goal is to lessen human suffering and progress well-being. Its values include:

- love, mindfulness and compassion
- trust and integrity
- teamwork and collaboration
- impeccability and continuous improvement
- open communication and transparency

The Mind and Life Institute sees the potential of a world that fully comprehends the importance of training the mind in ways that reduce suffering and support individual and planetary peace, health, well-being and collaboration. It also hopes that everyone will have access to mental and emotional health practices. To reach this goal, it is involved in scientific research to understand how humans can coach their minds to develop the qualities of mind described in the values above. The institute holds regular meetings to discuss its findings, which are also published.

The Board of Directors includes His Holiness the 14th Dalai Lama, Professor Richard Davidson, Dr Daniel Goleman and Dr Jon Kabat-Zinn.

Practice: Loving kindness meditation (Metta)

This meditation is the last practice the Buddha recommended to his students. It may be the most important one for you and your emotional well-being, and it is a very powerful tool for transformation. There are many different versions. You are invited to change the wording of this practice until it feels right and you can 'own' the words and feel they are congruent with your type of thinking and communication.

Before you start, find a quiet place and make sure you are warm and comfortable. It may be helpful to think of a compassionate story or experience so that you can create the feeling of love and empathy in your heart. Now let go of the story and visualize in the centre of your chest, your 'emotional' heart, an image of yourself as you are now or as you were as a little child, perhaps supported by a loving other. If visualizing is difficult for you, then try just seeing your name written in the centre of your heart.

The Metta practice starts with the pure intention wishing to increase self-compassion from within. It is rather like planting a seed, which will grow with regular practice.

Slowly, day by day and week by week, expand the practice. In week two, after meditating on ourselves, we add somebody we love and care for:

'May you be safe and protected.'

"May you be peaceful."

'May you live at ease and with kindness.'

'May I be safe and protected.'

"May I be peaceful."

'May I live at ease and with kindness.'

We finally expand the practice still further to include people we hardly know, people who may have caused us irritation or hurt:

'May all beings be safe and protected.'

"May all beings be peaceful.'

'May all beings live at ease and with kindness.'

Metta starts with the mere intention of loving kindness, and persistence in this practice can wonderfully deepen our experience of life, joy and meaning. If every one of us just managed to touch one 'other' through this practice, the world would indeed be a safer, kinder and more peaceful place in which to live.

So, if you want to keep it really simple, try something like this:

'I wish to be protected from harm.'

"I wish to be peaceful and happy.'

'I wish to be kind and compassionate.'

It may be enough just to visualize yourself and repeatedly think words such as 'peace', 'kindness', 'protection' and 'safety'. Don't let any complicated word structures get in the way of your intention. You could also visualize symbols that represent your intention instead of words: maybe a heart (for kindness and compassion), holding the hand of a friend (for safety), or seeing a loved one smile (for joy). For harmony, visualize a peacemaker such as Gandhi (or somebody known only to you) or a white dove. Be as creative as possible, and keep practising.

Sue's story

The following story illustrates how a compassionate monk passed on wisdom and invited somebody who was suffering to give compassion to others in order to learn self-compassion. He knew by experience that this would help his visitor more than anything else he could offer her. The research described earlier in this chapter also shows that when we engage in compassion for others the areas in the brain responsible for self-compassion become stronger, and vice versa.

Sue had been suffering for several years from a disease that caused her muscles to wither. Not only did she become more and more dependent on an electric wheelchair, but she also experienced excruciating pain, every day, all day long. Western medicine had nothing more to offer her.

So, when a friend told her about a Tibetan monk who was briefly visiting her town, she became excited at the possibility of finding comfort. He was well known for his Tibetan Dur Bon Medicine training and for great success in healing cases where Western medicine had been unsuccessful. She arranged a meeting with the monk. When she arrived, he smiled kindly and she started telling him about her years of suffering. After a while, he gently interrupted her. His message to her was simple: 'Focus less on your own suffering but make it your intention to help at least one other being that is suffering every day.' She felt rather cross for having received nothing but this piece of advice.

On her way home, she had to go shopping. She could just about manage it by carrying a little basket on her knees and reaching for produce on the lower shelves. When she arrived at the checkout, there was quite a long queue. The woman immediately behind her started complaining that there were never enough tills open and that she always ended up in the slowest queue, particularly when she had barely any time for shopping. Soon the whining woman had become the centre of attention for the whole shop. Sue noticed feeling irritated with her. She thought to herself: 'At least you can still rush.' Sue experienced self-pity and judgement towards that woman. Yet there was also a wise part of herself reminding her that she 'whined' rather often too. She wondered how that must come across to her family and friends. Suddenly, she also remembered the monk's recommendation. So Sue surprised herself when she said to the woman behind her: 'Why don't you go first? I'm not in a rush.'

It was at this point that the woman noticed Sue for the first time. She blushed when Sue turned round to her and became very apologetic, telling her that she had an important meeting to attend and that somebody in her family was sick. Sue felt compassion with her and found herself smiling and repeating that she really did not mind waiting. Slowly, she noticed that she had a warm, soothing feeling in the centre of her heart. When the woman had paid, thanked her and was gone, everybody in the supermarket nearby started applauding and thanking Sue. She was overwhelmed by the kindness and smiles from others.

This was only the beginning of Sue's journey into compassion and self-compassion. The more she gave to others, the healthier she felt. The pain she experienced gradually subsided, and she could also move more and more. Her recovery is ongoing, as is the compassion in her heart for all beings.

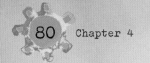

Pippa's story

Pippa was an extraordinary girl. As soon as she could utter sounds, she started singing songs and even composing some. She claims that in her own head she has seen bands of colours that came out as streams of music. She soon realized that she was very limited – after all, she could only hum one voice at a time. So she asked very early on to learn the violin, as she had observed that it was possible to play several strings at once.

In 1970, she heard Jacqueline du Pré (1945–1987) play the famous Elgar Cello Concerto. Now this was to be her fate: the cello. As soon as she was given her first cello at the age of five, she changed into an 'energy' that lived in and around the instrument. Many excellent teachers taught her and wondered whether she would surpass her inspiration. In 1973, though, Jacqueline was diagnosed with multiple sclerosis and slowly lost her gift.

Pippa was very sad about Jacqueline, but she had different ideas anyway about playing the cello. She wanted use the instrument in completely new ways, not just to play regular cello music. She used it as a drum, played it with her toes, sang into it, and so on. Everybody loved what she did, and famous musicians wrote pieces for her. She started travelling the globe and composing music herself.

She loved her work, and yet she was always fearful that she might lose her gift, as Jacqueline had done.

The cumbersome travels and her own sensitivity, mixed with jet lag, made her more and more unsettled. She became very unhappy but was only diagnosed with depression after her first attempt to take her own life. She was admitted to a hospital, and, even though she was in a secure ward, she managed to jump out of a window, which almost killed her. For four years, she had to be locked up and could not play her beloved instrument.

She met a new psychiatrist who said that meditation would be a means by which she could reconnect to her self. She went to a famous and wonderful place – Kagyu Samyé Ling Monastery and Tibetan Centre, near Dumfries and Galloway, Scotland – where she particularly connected to compassion meditation. The more she practised, the more the veil of fear and the feeling of being lost disappeared.

By the time I met her on a compassion retreat, she had been meditating for four years and had started playing her cello again. She gave all participants a free concert and produced a new compact disc for the meditation centre. She said that 'compassion' had saved her life.

5 Healthy attachment and self-acceptance

Are human beings hard-wired to be selfish, arrogant, mean and defensive, or could early experiences of feeling loved and accepted be responsible for how we feel and behave towards others in later life?

Why is it that people who feel emotionally safe and secure seem to act more compassionately towards other beings? Having sensitive, available and empathic parents or carers helps children's self-confidence and makes them less prone to being anxious or egotistic. If a child feels psychologically safe, they will be comfortable showing closeness, affection and trust towards others. Safely attached people are much less likely to suffer from depression than those who experienced anxious or detached parenting.

Children have a psychological need to feel safe and protected. So when our carers provide us with positive learning and nurture experiences, we build up a sense of well-being, resilience and self-acceptance, which are essential 'ingredients' in a human being's emotional and mental growth. The author and psychologist Kristin Neff, a world expert in the field of self-compassion, calls our need for attachment and care the 'tend and befriend' instinct.

Parents, or other adults who raise us, are in principle vital for our survival. Most mammals need the care and protection of their parent(s) in order to make it into adulthood (this is known as the 'attachment system'). Humans are the most vulnerable species. Young monkeys can and will, should their mother die or reject them, cling onto other females until one allows them to stay and starts treating them as their offspring. A human baby obviously cannot do that – it is utterly dependent and at the mercy of somebody else.

It is our 'birthright' to receive affection and connection with others. If you get only minimal support, or are only 'noticed' when you get something wrong, you grow up feeling judged and maybe even worthless. As our 'hard disk' (brain memory) is virtually empty when we are born (we have fewer instincts than other mammals), we store whatever we learn, and the early learned patterns leave the deepest grooves in our memory.

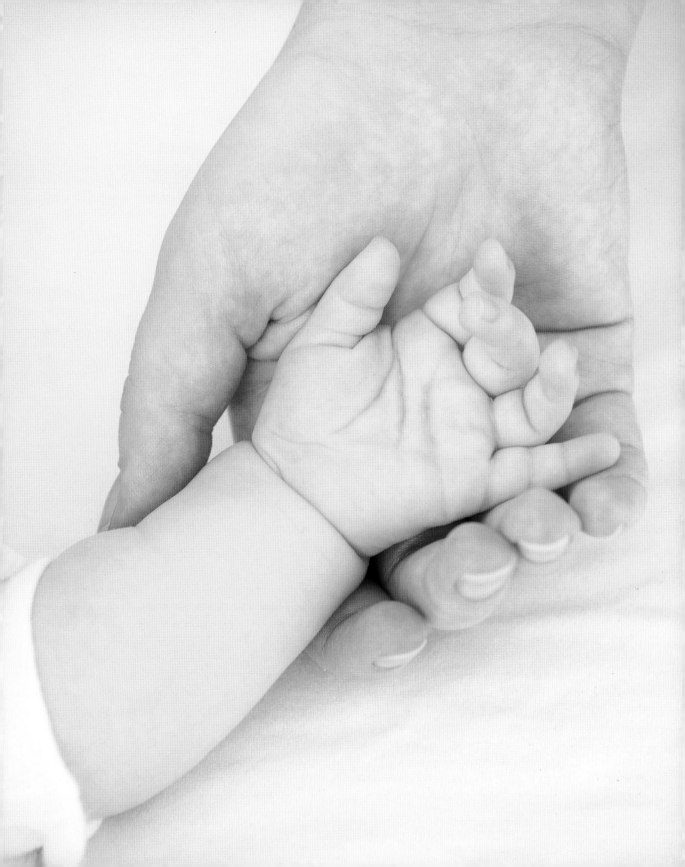

So, having overcritical carers, or ones who can barely look after themselves (such as parents with mental health problems or addictions), will create in our awareness beliefs and behaviours that are learned by observing and experiencing inept patterns. Thus, we may continue treating ourselves with ongoing criticism, long after our carers have moved out of our lives. If we experienced our parents as being incompetent, and in particular if we had to care for them when we should have been cared for, we tend to feel that nobody can be trusted and we have to do it all ourselves. When we experience neglect, rejection, abandonment and other traumas, these experiences leave mental marks and scars.

The fantastic news, however, is that our brains are 'plastic', which simply means that they have the capacity to change. If we learn to give ourselves the nurture and kindness we continually need, we will be able to create new thinking and behaviour patterns.

Here are a few practices that will help you lessen the wounds of the past and create a new, self-accepting you.

Practice: Give yourself a good hug

Have you ever noticed how children who feel upset or bullied sit down on the floor and wrap their arms around their knees? They may even rock forwards and backwards to soothe themselves, just like they may have been rocked by their parents when they were tiny babies.

So, when you feel upset or lonely, wrap your arms around your chest and squeeze yourself a little, or stroke your upper arms for a while, as you would do when feeling cold.

Research at Rosock and Justus-Liebig Universities in Germany, among others, has shown that this type of self-care releases the chemical oxytocin. This chemical reduces feelings of fear and increases a sense of protection, bonding and peace.

Edward the seducer

Edward was extremely intelligent, attractive and charming. He finished his PhD in Philosophy when he was 25 and was invited to teach at his university. This only lasted for a few years, however, as Edward had two significant problems. First, he tended to seduce most women of reasonable looks and intelligence, and this included his female colleagues, his male colleagues' girlfriends and wives, and, occasionally, a student. After only three years, he lost his job after a student reported him as 'stalking' her. Of course, he disputed the whole story, but in the end everybody was glad to see him go. He had been a fascinating person and an inspiring lecturer, but he knew no boundaries.

This led to a severe recurrence of his second problem: he became very depressed and even suicidal. He attempted to take his own life, but was rescued in time. The interesting thing about Edward was that as soon as he felt looked after – and all the nurses wanted to look after Edward as much as the female doctors did – he started his game of seduction all over again. During the month he spent in hospital, he broke at least three hearts.

He received psychotherapy while on the in-house treatment programme. The therapist was male and extremely compassionate and patient. He learned that Edward had suffered from depression since his teenage years and also from a certain 'wanderlust' when it came to women. He never had a problem making contact and being intimate. In this department, his skills were excellent. Yet he always got a very strong urge to run away when a woman confessed she loved him or was falling in love with him. Hearing the word 'love' brought shivers to his spine.

The therapist had an insight: perhaps Edward had experienced something traumatic to do with 'love' in his early cognitive and preverbal state of childhood. He asked Edward about his infant years and his parents. Edward told him that he never knew his father and that he had grown up with his mother and his grandparents. The grandparents were fervent Catholics and never bonded with him. They had allowed their daughter and the 'bastard' to live with them until she could support herself. His mum was 16 years old when he was born.

Edward's grandparents punished their daughter by completely ignoring her and Edward, and by never helping out or babysitting. So this young girl had to give up school and do her best to bring up Edward on her own. The therapist thought this was significant. He wondered whether Edward had felt loved and secure as a little boy. Edward drew a blank. He had not seen his mother in years (viewing her as another woman who deserved to be abandoned) and had no idea whether she loved him. The therapist suggested that Edward write her a letter asking her to join one therapy session. Edward resisted for a long time, but the therapist eventually convinced him that some important data could be collected from the one person who knew him well in his early developmental years.

His mother was actually very touched and pleased to help Edward. In the session she said she had missed him so much during the last years, and that she had always felt guilty about not being a good daughter or mother. The therapist asked her whether she ever told Edward that she loved him when he was a little boy, and she hesitated. The therapist gently invited her to share what this hesitation was about. She said, with tears in her eyes: 'Yes, I often told him that I loved him and that he was my precious baby boy, but at the time I actually did not really mean it. I was anxious about my future, I was angry about my parents punishing me, I was frustrated about having to give up school and about Edward's dad never supporting me at all. So I often said loving things but deep in my heart I hated him for all the troubles his arrival had caused.' At this point, Edward and his mum were both crying. Now it was obvious why Edward always ran away from 'love'. He must have sensed the hatred and rejection when his mum used the word 'love', and it triggered in him the need to run away, as its meaning was so very different for him than from the women in his life who had declared their love for him.

The therapist, with their permission, held their hands and asked them to participate in an intervention, which might help both of them let go of the past hurt and guilt. So the three held hands in a circle, and mother and son were asked to close their eyes. The therapist asked them to return mentally to a place of safety when Edward was around three years of age. They both nodded and agreed on the little garden behind the grandparents' house. The therapist asked them to visualize themselves sitting on a blanket with the mother holding her boy and stroking his hair. After a while, the therapist asked Edward's mum to imagine seeing her mature self standing behind her (invisible to Edward) and supporting her to use the right words while stroking his head. The adult self also told her young self to really feel in her heart all the love she now felt for Edward. It was very moving how she actually said to him how sorry she was for her mistakes, but how very much she loved him and that he was the best gift she had ever received. By now Edward's mum had actually started to gently

touch and stroke his hair and he was leaning on her shoulder. The therapist allowed this compassionate healing to unfold and last as long as they needed.

After a while, Edward opened his eyes and sat up straight and said: 'Thank you, Mum. That felt so good.' She totally agreed. The therapist explained to both of them that this was the beginning of a journey where their attachment to love and for acceptance of each other could grow, and new thinking and feeling structures would develop in their minds.

Mother and son both started afresh, and slowly Edward learned – by allowing his mother to express her love for him – to let the word 'love' take on a new meaning in a relationship he started with a woman around a year after this poignant therapy session. He still needed his therapist to help him deal with the deep-seated tendency to run away, but slowly he dissolved this now unnecessary urge.

Practice: Compassionate breath

1   Sit in an upright position and feel your feet firmly
    grounded on the floor. Maybe wrap a shawl or
    blanket around your shoulders so that you feel snug
    and warm. Cross your hands in front of your heart.

2   Visualize yourself as an innocent child or, if it is
    easier, any innocent child.

3   Bring your awareness to your breathing. Breathing
    in, notice how the breath travels down into your
    chest area and even further down into your
    abdomen. Then there is a little natural pause before
    the breath is released and travels back up and out
    of your nostrils. I generally recommend breathing
    in and out through your nostrils. If, however, you
    have a cold, or for any other reason, have to breathe
    in through your mouth, make the opening of your
    mouth small and gently breathe in. On the out-
    breath, imagine you are blowing onto a spoon full
    of hot soup and you don't want to spill any – this
    will simulate nostril breathing. Continue focusing
    on your natural in and out breathing for a while
    until you feel more and more settled.

4   Now start focusing on 'the little child in your
    heart'. What would you like to say to him or her?
    Allow compassionate, warm words and phrases to
    arise in your mind, as if you were trying to calm
    an upset little one. I prefer not to prescribe the
    language to use. I hope you can just stay with
    your heart and allow kind words to arise.

5   After a while, return to your breathing. Slowly
    put your hands down on your lap and continue
    breathing for a little longer.

Practice: Visualization – feeling safe with your benefactor

Remember the need for a healthy 'attachment system'? It is active throughout our life, informing every relationship we have and how we respond to difficulties. If we are able to bond with others and trust them, we will cope much better when life is challenging. So, if you can visualize someone who cares for you, even if that person is no longer alive, this symbolic protector can quickly help you soothe yourself when difficulties arise. This practice is particularly helpful when you feel frightened or anxious.

1   Lie down or sit, covering yourself with a shawl or blanket.

2   Visualize yourself in your favourite place of safety, such as a meadow, a room, a garden.

3   Now see the person who creates a sense of safety for you walk towards you with open arms. When they have arrived, they give you a hug or hold your hands. Internally, hear them say the words 'safety', 'protection' and 'peace'; or if you prefer, let them talk or sing a soothing lullaby to you.

4   Put your hand on your heart centre and stay with this visualization as long as you wish.

The animal kingdom and compassion

Having looked at how humans can develop a sense of safety and self-acceptance, even later on in life through the practice of self-compassion and loving kindness, it may interest you to learn about other mammals and how they use and apply their sense and need for attachment. There are many wonderful stories in which animals, pets and others have helped either humans or species other than their own.

Did you know that we share 99 per cent of our DNA with chimpanzees, 98 per cent with gorillas and 97 per cent with orang-utans? We even share approximately 60 per cent with felines, so it is not too far-fetched to say that all life has a common source. Only humans, who are considered to be the species with the highest intellect, sometimes forget that this planet belongs to all forms of life. The 'Metta' practice (see page 76) emphasizes that we want safety, protection, peace and ease for all beings.

There is a very unusual story of a lion that repeatedly adopted antelopes and defended them against other lions.

Dogs have been known to care for cats, ducks and squirrels. There are cats that cared for rats, chimps that looked after cats, and one chimp in particular that became the surrogate mother of two white baby tigers. She played with them, stroked them and even fed them with a bottle. Can you believe that there was a fully grown Bengal tiger that became the adoptive mother of six piglets, or a 130-year-old tortoise that cared for a baby hippo?

Many more animals are known to care compassionately for their own species when sick or wounded, and this behaviour is not largely based on reciprocity. Fables and stories that tell of animals such as wolves or apes adopting lost children in jungles, and cinema movies like *Jungle Book* and *Tarzan* have mesmerized audiences all over the world. Here are three stories in which animals' altruistic and compassionate behaviour saved human lives. The first involves dolphins.

Near the Australian Great Barrier Reef, a family used to swim regularly from one beach to another. The swim usually lasted a good half-hour, and the father took his three teenagers almost daily since they all aspired to become 'beach-safe' and lifeguards. On one of these outings, one daughter and one son had almost reached their destination when they turned round and saw their dad and sister being circled by a big white shark. The father held tightly on to his daughter, so they would appear to be a larger target, and they hoped that the shark would leave them alone. But not so! However, only a few minutes into this horror, a school of dolphins started circling the shark, creating an outer ring. Occasionally, individual dolphins even stabbed the shark with their snouts, and more and more joined in. Dolphins have been known to attack and even kill sharks, so after ten minutes or so the shark simply left and the dolphins accompanied the father and daughter right up to the shore, until they were safe.

The second story is about a dog. M had been fighting in the Gulf War when he was seriously wounded. He lost the use of his legs, and also most of his memory. When he woke up from this nightmare, he was in a wheelchair and did not recognize his wife or his children. He was also unable to tap into his emotions and just felt numb. One day he went to visit a guide dog training camp, and there was one particular Labrador that had been very unresponsive to the training and was considered to be difficult. When M dropped a glove, however, the dog ran over and picked it up and put it in his lap. M did not praise or thank him. The dog seemed to try again; he went over to the drinks stall, grabbed a tin and brought it back to M in the same fashion. M says that at that moment something seemed to reconnect in his brain, and he felt a warm, fuzzy feeling in his heart and patted the Labrador. The emotional centre of the brain seemingly reopened and M smiled for the first time since he had been injured.

Research shows that humans and pets alike create oxytocin – this is the same chemical produced by lactating mothers when feeding their babies – so the feeling of love is reciprocated. A scientific study shows that stroking a dog or a cat can have a very similar effect on your mood as being around your infant. Miho Nagasawa and Takefumi Kikusui, who are biologists at Azuba University in Japan, conducted a series of tests to see if close contact between two species can produce oxytocin. They concluded that the hormone is released in similar quantities in both cases, triggering happiness, stress and depression relief, as well as an increased feeling of trust. The chemical also makes it possible to bond, which is essential for survival in humans.

M kept the Labrador and this changed his life completely. For whatever reason, this dog loved his keeper and felt his needs. He helped him with all the activities M could no longer achieve by himself, even posting letters and getting money out of a cashpoint machine. He reunited M with his wife and children. M had become withdrawn and very depressed. His life felt worthless to him now. But his family loved the dog and so did he and so they ended up loving each other again. M renewed his marriage vows and was the happiest he could be within the constraints of his new circumstances. Then one day he and his wife were on a pavement when a reckless driver lost control and knocked them both down. When M regained consciousness he noticed that the Labrador had turned him onto his side so he could breathe properly, brought him his mobile phone and then run to the nearby pub to look for help. The dog saved two lives that evening.

Years later, when the beloved animal was dying in his arms, M gave him a last gift – the gift of tears and sadness which had still been locked up until then.

The last story is not only almost unbelievable, but it may even enable improvements in human medical diagnosis. Over a period of two or three weeks, Anne noticed that her ten-year-old dog Scruffy had become listless and almost unresponsive. She feared that he was very ill and might die soon. Whenever she leaned down to stroke him, however, he sniffed around her left chest area and seemed to get agitated. She had discovered a lump in her left breast but the doctor said it was a cyst and nothing to worry about.

Scruffy kept repeating his strange behaviour, and one day Anne just knew that the diagnosis was wrong. She went back to the hospital and had a mammogram, but nothing looked suspicious. Only when she demanded that a sample was removed from the 'cyst' did the doctors realize that Anne was right. It was cancer. As soon as she had completed her treatment, Scruffy was his old self again, and still is. Research by Carolyn M Willis and her colleagues, reported in the *British Medical Journal* in 2004, shows that dogs can smell cancer in people's urine and may soon be used for non-invasive diagnoses.

Compassion should ideally expand further than our concern for human life. It can be one of our most crucial virtues and there are so many moments when we could express it to all living beings around us.

Practice: Connect with the animal world

This is for those who feel a deep connection to creatures, big and small. Write down in your journal what you would like to do to express compassion for animals. Here are some ideas.

- The animal world would greatly benefit from your support. Maybe you could help out in an animal rescue centre, or – if you don't have the time – why not donate funds to it?
- Adopt an animal through an endangered species trust or charity.
- Drive mindfully to avoid killing animals on the road.
- If you don't love insects, at least bear with them. Did you know that spiders like to eat mosquitoes? So don't just squash them.
- Never litter the environment, since by doing so you are destroying the natural habitat of our animal friends.

Do you have any more insightful and compassionate ideas?

6 Learning to forgive

As you may remember from previous chapters, self-compassion and compassion for others are closely linked. A definition of compassion could be 'the ability to suffer with others', and in self-compassion applying the same respect and kindness to ourselves when we are experiencing pain and trials.

The human condition exposes us to challenges that we sometimes meet with bravery and honesty, but at other times bring out the worst in us and others. When we or others act unkindly, selfishly or without thinking of the larger picture – acknowledging that we are all (including nature and beasts) deeply connected and interdependent – it is sometimes difficult to feel the warm kindness in our heart that could be there. In order to really feel compassion and open to its powerful gateway, we may need to forgive ourselves or others first. Guilt and shame towards ourselves, or anger and hatred towards others, are destructive emotions that hinder us in deepening self-compassion and compassion towards others. We need to let go of such negative emotions as much as we can.

Forgiveness cannot be forced but, just like 'loving kindness' (Metta), it can evolve from a tiny seed of intention and grow by persistently opening ourselves to it. This is far from condoning negative actions. We are, however, forgiving the misunderstanding and bewilderment on our part that may have caused them. Thus, we may even learn from the past and avoid re-enacting similar hurtful deeds.

Human compassion, or what I sometimes call 'human affection', is the key factor for all human business.

His Holiness the 14th Dalai Lama (1935–)

Jack Kornfield tells a wonderful tale in his book *The Art of Forgiveness, Lovingkindness, and Peace* (Bantam, 2002), about a fundamentally different approach to handling unkind behaviour – a ritual of forgiveness. A tribe in South Africa called the Bambemba use kindness to help a perpetrator re-enter their society. They put him in the middle of the village. Everyone stops going about their daily routines and work and joins a circle around him. Now they do something rather unusual. Every single member of the tribe in the circle tells the guilty one about a good action they remember him being involved in during his whole life. It could go back to his childhood or something he recently did. All his helpful actions and strengths are remembered and recited. This ritual can go on for days. Finally, the circle opens and all the villagers have a party together where they celebrate the rebirth of their brother/sister.

Can you imagine how healing such an encounter could be? You know that you have done something unkind and yet you are reminded only of all your good actions. It is a certain recipe for being enabled to let go of shame and guilt and feel totally held and supported by all your significant others. It may even stop your own negative self-talk and help you reconnect to all that is good and lovable within you.

Real forgiveness can only be reached if we are able to drop our relentless standards that nobody could ever really measure up to. Rick Hanson, an American neuropsychologist, puts it beautifully: 'Seeing faults clearly, taking responsibility for them with remorse and making amends, and then coming to peace about them: this is what I mean by forgiving yourself.'

Equally important is the ability to forgive others for wrong actions and behaviours. It can be easy to feel compassion when others are hurting. However, when they have hurt us, our heart needs to expand and reach out into darkness and thunder and go beyond our comfort zone in order to express compassion.

The author and psychologist Kristin Neff conducted an experiment that concluded that self-compassionate people found it easier to forgive others who had pained them. If you can see that the flaws of others might mirror your own transgressions, you may find the kindness it takes to let go of annoyance, anger and blame.

Releasing resentment will lighten your own being and could help the one who offended you to gain insight and start again. Of course, it depends on the harshness of the offence whether you wish to continue having a relationship with the other. Self-compassion may mean 'yes' to forgiving, but 'no' to continuing to engage with the person who hurt you.

I remember a sad, yet wonderful, story where a mother who lost her son Jo to a gun crime actually started visiting in prison the boy who had committed the deed. She was heartbroken and yet she knew that her son's death had been an accident. Jo had also carried a gun, and after a drunken night out the two adolescents had been fooling around with their guns. It ended in the terrible fact that one of them lay dead in the street. She reckoned it could have been the other way round. Both

of them had actually purchased their guns illegally. The young man she visited weekly, who had been sentenced for the illegal possession of firearms and accidental killing, was full of remorse. She had known him for years. Jo and he had been friends since childhood. He had often visited them, as his parents were dead and his grandmother was often busy looking after four grandchildren.

The more often she visited him in prison, the deeper her compassion for him grew. He was so low and so sad, but equally her visits kept him going. After four years in prison, he was released and the mother said he could move in with her if he wanted to. This was her final act of true kindness and forgiveness – she welcomed him home as if he were her own son.

Practice: Forgiving someone who pained you

Wait until you feel truly ready to forgive; give it time and thought. Bring to awareness the reasons that may have led the other to do what they did.

1   Consider what might have caused the harm you experienced. What emotions could have been present when the other acted: anxiety, misunderstanding, anger, envy, stress? Without condoning the act, can you see that under the circumstances you or somebody else you deeply care for might have done the same? What may have been going on in the other's mind, so that they could not control their actions? Maybe their stress had temporarily affected their emotional awareness and they acted 'without thinking'. Perhaps they did not have the privilege of good parenting or education. What if they actually were simply inconsiderate, self-centred and vicious? Had they themselves been treated harshly, or might they have a genetic predisposition that led to their behaviour?

2   Now that you have searched your heart and mind for explanations, maybe the only option in order to free yourself and them from everlasting resentment is to accept their human flaws. Freeing yourself from the poisonous feelings of ongoing anger may help you to think 'forgiveness' and let go of blame. Take small steps if the offence was vast. The Metta meditation (see page 76), wishing the other well, can be really helpful here, as can patience towards your own feelings of hurt and vulnerability.

3   Now it is your turn. Can you actually find it within you to accept that your behaviour can be flawed and yet you are a beautiful part of creation?

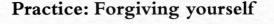

Practice: Forgiving yourself

Use your notebook and work through the following.

1 Write down those deeds for which you feel you need forgiveness. What do you want to be aware of so that you may be really able to absolve yourself? Be prepared to work on one issue at a time.

2 After writing it all down, try to imagine someone else in your shoes. Maybe you know somebody who has been unkind to you. What would the other feel? Would you be able to forgive that person? Invite the wisest and most kind-hearted part of you to forgive that confused and maybe guilty person.

3 Now try to tune into the wholesome compassion you just created. You could even use some phrases from the 'loving kindness' (Metta) meditation (see page 76): 'Let me be safe, let me be peaceful and kind.' Apply the same kindness and open-heartedness to yourself and the erroneous behaviour that you no longer want to condone.

4 Write down (and congratulate yourself for) all your kind, brave and beneficial actions that you can remember. You may find it helpful to visualize somebody who loves you and hear them tell you what is great about you.

Be patient and work through your list one step at a time. You may need to go through one or more of the steps a few times so you can truly forgive yourself. Allow the experience of being forgiven to take some time to sink in. Open up to it in your body and heart. Feel the freedom and lightness that come with the removal of guilt and with the remembrance of kindness. How does that feel in your body? How do you think you and others will benefit from you forgiving yourself and feeling free?

Transgressions

All that we ought to have thought and have not thought;
All that we ought to have spoken and have not spoken;
All that we ought to have done and have not done;
All that we ought not to have thought and yet have thought;
All that we ought not to have spoken and yet have spoken;
All that we ought not to have done and yet have done;
For thoughts, words and works, pray we, O God, for
    forgiveness,
And repent with penance.

> From the *Zend-Avesta*
> (6th century BC),
> a Zoroastrian text, Persia

Love in Forgiveness

I forgive you for what you have said and done.
I forgive you for what you believe to be true.
I forgive you for making light of the hurt you have caused.
I forgive you for not saying sorry.
I do not withhold my love.
If I ever do so, please forgive me.

> Modern prayer from Tel Aviv,
> Israel

Learning to forgive mum

Once there was a little girl called Kirsty. She was a kind and gentle spirit and her mum loved her very much. She totally adored her mum, too. Often Kirsty would wear her mum's beautiful underskirts, which were made of silk and silver threads, and then she put on her pearls and shoes and walked around saying that she really was a princess. Of course, for her mum she was a princess anyway. Kirsty was also quite clever and her mum taught her to read, sing, swim and ski before she was four years old. Everybody was impressed, or so it seemed.

Kirsty also had a dad, and he might have loved her, too, but she was never quite sure. He was very strict and had many rules. When he wanted to sleep after lunch, Kirsty had to be absolutely quiet for an hour. When he wanted to watch his programmes on TV, whatever Kirsty was watching was simply switched over, and every weekend they drove to Kirsty's granny who looked after her on Saturday and Sunday. Kirsty always dreaded the journey, because her dad smoked in the car which made Kirsty very sick. Even though her mum pleaded with her dad not to smoke, he did it anyway.

When Kirsty was about five years old, her mum began to change. She started to drink some brown liquid from the bottles in the living room cabinet. Afterwards, she always asked Kirsty to help her refill the bottles with black tea, which looked just like the brown liquid that mum had drunk before. It was an exciting game, and Kirsty had to promise not to tell dad.

One day, dad brought back a visitor and they both drank some of the brown liquid. Mum was hiding in the kitchen. When the visitor left, dad was very cross with mum. They were screaming at each other and mum threw a heavy glass ashtray at dad. It missed him and ripped a painting on the wall before it shattered on the floor. Kirsty helped to tidy up. Soon her mum was sent away to see a doctor in a sanatorium and Kirsty stayed with one aunt, then another aunt, and with her granny at the weekends.

She was so happy when mum returned home and seemed a lot better. But it did not last very long. Kirsty came home from school at three o'clock and mum was not even dressed but was lying on the floor, not moving. Kirsty could not wake her up, so she called for an ambulance. It came very quickly and her mum was taken away to the hospital again. Kirsty had to stay with the aunts and with her granny, and she really missed her mum. Dad was very busy with his work and she did not see him often.

For many years, Kirsty experienced this terrible pain in her chest; it felt as if it would burst. She was always frightened when she returned home after school, for she never knew how mum would be and, more often than not, she was very odd. She would talk strangely, not cook any more, and hide the bottles with the brown liquid that Kirsty hated the smell of.

The worst day was when mum jumped out of the window. Kirsty thought she would never see her again, but mum must have had a guardian angel, for she landed on the balcony below and not five floors down on the road. Mum survived but needed many operations and was away for three months. Then dad wanted to leave mum, but in the end he didn't. Kirsty grew up into a young woman herself and was looking after mum who never really recovered.

So, is there a happy end to this tale? Maybe, but maybe not – it depends on how you look at it. When Kirsty's dad died, her mum stopped drinking, just like that. She was an old woman now, quite unwell and frightened. But one day she told Kirsty about her life and why she had escaped into the other world that the brown liquid opened to her. She told Kirsty about her own childhood and how she had lost her beloved father when she was only 10 years old, and how a man had abused her when she was only 14. She told Kirsty that the happiest years were those when she first met dad and then had her little daughter. But, after a few years of marriage, dad's business grew and he liked other women, too, and mum had just not known what to do. So what she did was drink alcohol and forget.

She asked Kirsty to forgive her. She asked her many, many times, telling her, like in the old days, how much she loved her and how proud she was of her. Kirsty did her best and started to forgive and is still forgiving her each day, month, year … one step at a time.

…one step at a time.

Joan Puls, a Sister of the Order of St Francis, wrote a wonderful book entitled *A Spirituality of Compassion* (Twenty-Third Publications, 1988) in order to assist interfaith dialogue. Some of her ideas are really helpful when we address the issue of forgiveness.

At the vulnerable age of 13, Joan was repeatedly abused by a priest. She buried those episodes and carried them with her for almost two decades. Then, during therapy, they surfaced. She realized that part of her continued growth depended on removing the anger and resentment that she still felt towards the priest. She describes the feeling of release she experienced after she wrote the honest letter to him, informing him of the damage he had inflicted upon her. Although the priest never replied, she says: 'Each of us must find ways to unblock the streams of life that have been clogged by past traumas and long forgotten wounds.' Forgiveness is therapeutic.

Finding true forgiveness

Forgiveness may come easily when the relationship involved is casual and not very meaningful. It is uncomplicated if it does not entail too much giving up of what you are attached to, such as your views or possessions. Some forms of forgiveness, such as having to go to church for confession or asking children who had a fight to say 'sorry', can feel like an obligation, and may be only a matter of ritual absolution.

Without genuine acceptance of the other person, forgiveness will be shallow and superficial – 'I forgive you, but do you realize how deeply you have wounded me?' Genuine acceptance comes when we acknowledge our limited understanding, especially of the other's motives, and recognize the contributing causes we bring to a conflict. Part of this process of accepting and forgiving is to realize our own potential for wounding and inflicting pain on others, even on those we love.

Jonathan Graham, an aspiring pastor and teacher from South Carolina, shares: 'He who first made the breathtaking discovery that at the heart of the universe is love … learned this secret … from the breaking of his own heart.' As such, forgiving is an active practice. By forgiving others, we acknowledge that each of us is both wounder and wounded. Without forgiveness, we would stay in the illusion of fixed roles, one being the offender and the other the offended.

Forgiveness always occurs within the context of pain. It asks us to deepen our understanding, to open the borders around our heart, to live with a new degree of tolerance. It is a bending of our heart, a giving up of our self-proclaimed righteousness, all of which is costly. It means letting go of our attachment to our natural reactions: humiliation, anger, deep hurt, suspicion, mistrust. As such, it is also freeing us, the one who forgives.

Sometimes we have to forgive life and its events, let go of our questions and demand for answers. If we don't, we close ourselves off from the beauty and enjoyment life has to offer, even in a time of grief and bewilderment.

Forgiveness is a daily challenge: to let go of our desire to control life, to let go of our need to direct outcomes and pre-plan the movements of ourselves and those around us, to let go of some of our expectations of others, to let go of weather forecasts, the unscheduled interruption, the unexpected illness. If we cannot live at peace amid the disruptions and inadequacies of our daily surroundings, we will hardly be ready to make peace with the more significant wounds and traumas of our life. These daily disturbances and challenges provide our training for larger moments in life such as offering the gift of forgiveness to someone just before he dies or asking for forgiveness in the same situation.

Forgiveness is to accept the pain caused and absorb it. It means discontinuing the battle, disarming ourselves. Forgiveness is very difficult because we confuse it with condoning as right something that felt wrong. It is difficult because it means we have to set aside our pride, our need to win and our desire to control or be right.

Can we forgive those who hold differing or opposing beliefs? Will we be able to surrender labels and stereotypes and recognize that the one quality we all have in common is our humanity? True forgiveness is an act of containing our pain and the refusal to turn it into hatred or revenge, so that healing can flow to the offender. The estrangement is transformed into reconciliation, the hostility into understanding. The writer and theologian Charles Williams (1886–1945) said that forgiveness is a re-identification with love, love revisited, love replanted, love recovered and love renamed.

Practice: Forgiving and asking for forgiveness

This practice is based on teachings by S.N. Goenka, who practises Buddhist Vipassan meditation. You can use it as a continuation of the first and second practices in this chapter (see pages 102 and 103), and slowly work your way through the different hurts you have received or caused.

1   Take a seat in a peaceful room, making sure you will be warm and undisturbed.

2   Now make contact with your heart – its ability to love, to be open, to be warm.

3   Bring to mind someone who has caused you pain, willingly or unwillingly, through thoughts, words or actions. Remember that those actions came from a place of not-knowing, illusion or stupidity, wanting to be happy as we all do, knowing that we all hurt others. Forgive this person, silently saying: 'I forgive you/May you be forgiven.'

4   Now remember that you have also caused pain to somebody, willingly or unwillingly, through thoughts, words or actions. Remember that those actions came from a place of not-knowing, and quietly ask this person to forgive you: 'May I be forgiven/Please forgive me.'

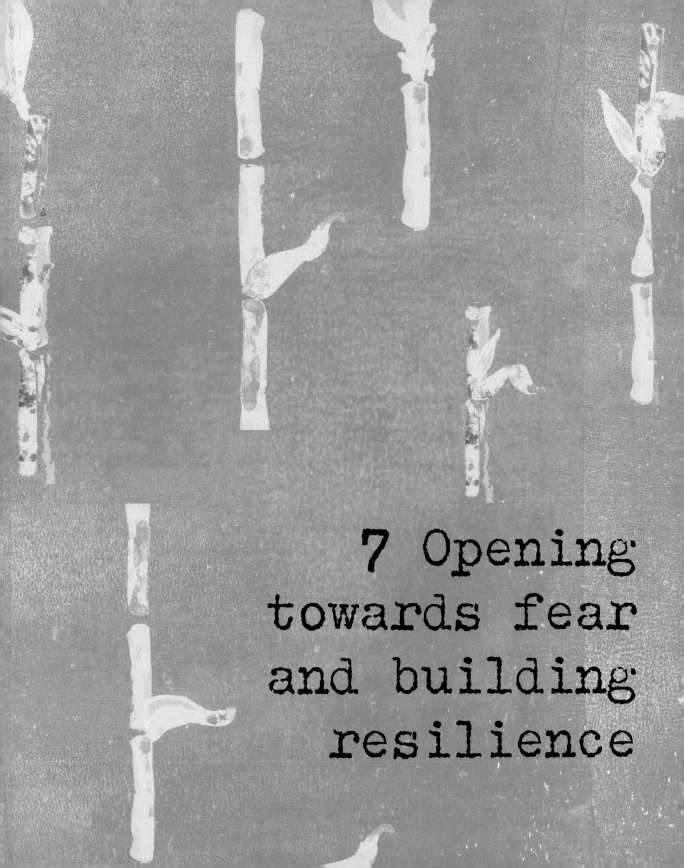

7 Opening towards fear and building resilience

SELF-COMPASSION IS ALSO NEEDED when considering your emotional state. Fear is one of the emotions that leads to a number of unhelpful, behavioural patterns lacking in compassion. Fear may hold us back from being creative or trying something new; fear can make us narrow-minded and reactive; and fear frequently leads humankind to destroy others.

If you are interested in this topic, you may be someone who experiences a particular type of fear, or who suffers from a number of different manifestations. Worry can often be like an infectious disease. If you don't cure one aspect of it, it will soon spread into other areas of your life. Does this sound familiar?

The key aim of this chapter is to lift the veil from the mysterious mind-state that is fear, and to offer you clear interventions in order to reduce its impact on you as much as possible. You will attempt to get to a level of acceptance where you can honestly say: 'I am feeling the fear still, but I am not going to let it stop me from leading my life.'

On a level of cognitive functioning, humans cannot be surpassed by any other species on Earth. However, we are structurally rather weak: we have no claws, huge teeth, heavy fur or scales to protect us. So, basically, we are very vulnerable, and thus have always had to be on high alert to avoid being eaten by a predator. Of course, it is true that our natural predators have reduced significantly in the 21st century. We have, though, created modern versions of creatures such as 'dinosaurs', 'sabre-toothed tigers' and 'mammoths' that cause our brain to go into overdrive! The new threats are machines, technology, speed, overpopulation, commuting and pollution, to name just a few.

Our threat-detection system does not know the difference between 'a demanding project we feel inadequate for' and a wild, man-eating cat. A few anxious thoughts and short breaths are enough to activate the 'fight or flight' response. All that has really changed are the triggers. Evolution has not assisted humans to feel calmer and less anxious when under pressure. As Paul Gilbert wisely pointed out in his book *The Compassionate Mind* (Constable, 2009), Mother Nature was purely focusing on helping our species survive, not on how to 'chill out' and have a good time.

Letting go of fear

We all know the typical physiological signs of anxiety – sweating, shaking, feeling paralysed, being unable to speak – but there are also much subtler ways in which your heart and mind express fear. Do you ever find yourself tuning off the world and instead switching on the television or a computer game? Before you know it, you are enveloped in a world where you watch but do not really participate. You won't be able to succeed there, but you definitely won't lose either. You are just there – like a one-celled organism in the ocean of life. Can you think of any other ways of avoiding engaging with life? Safe, isn't it? Nothing can go wrong, apart from the fact that life passes you by.

Human beings are pack animals. We mostly like doing things together. This is why so many people join a walking or running club, or a bowling or tennis group, because it is so much easier to 'get going' when we are not alone. Have you ever noticed giving yourself a hard time and telling yourself off for not having gone running or to the gym? Every time you do this, your memory adds another little negative bias towards those activities. All your brain can remember is that you were unhappy or even stressed when you were thinking of your chosen action. This will in the long run make it harder and harder to find the motivation to do it at all.

The underlying fear that leads to such procrastination can either be 'feeling all alone' or 'fearing failure'. In order to avoid feeling unpleasant sensations, we avoid 'doing it' altogether: the project, the piece of writing, the family dinner, the birthday party.

If you want to learn to befriend a destructive emotion such as fear, the first step is to mindfully accept it, just for now. When you manage to do this, sooner or later, and with the help of skilful thoughts and meditations, you will learn how to deal with it.

Let's start with small changes. The first is a basic willingness to engage in compassionate acts during your daily interaction with others. For example, in the morning when you still feel half asleep, you could say goodbye to your family and hello to a stranger in a shop or beside you on the train. You need not prepare for heroic gestures from the word go, but you will need to find the willingness to be really present and help out if a problem occurs around you. Opening a door for an old lady who is struggling with her shopping, stopping a football from rolling into the road for a schoolchild, giving words of kindness to colleagues who seem a little down, showing patience with another who may find a certain task difficult – all these acts show a willingness to let go of fear (of being rejected or not good at explaining) and open up to compassion. You are learning to listen to the cries of the world around you, even the silent ones. The more you do this, the more open-hearted you will become. Soon you will find yourself listening to the complaints of homeless people, or to the concerns of the colleague who always seemed in control but now suffers terribly after his daughter was diagnosed with cancer – his suffering and, in particular his sharing

it with you, has shown that he has his own struggles and demons and that he felt your compassionate heart.

A recent movie called *Mary and Martha* (written by Richard Curtis, 2013) brought two mothers together from different parts of the world. They had both lost their young sons to malaria. Their pain was unbearable, but by supporting each other they were able to rise above their own suffering and see that in Africa every day hundreds of children are afflicted and die from this disease. Out of compassion, the unlikely pair started campaigning and raising awareness for all the children affected by the disease, which can be prevented.

Why should we be so concerned with the suffering of others? Might we not challenge ourselves too much, as we are also not free from burden? When we are totally self-absorbed, we can easily become vulnerable to anxiety, but when we commit to alleviating the suffering of others, we may discover limitless courage and a readiness to offer relief to others.

Practice: Learn to avoid avoidance

Make a list in your notebook of the various ways in which you tend to 'avoid' life (and, by proxy, errors), through actions such as:

- constantly checking your mobile
- reading the paper from beginning to end ('Well, it is our duty, isn't it?')
- forgetting important dates with friends
- checking your emails once an hour
- listening to the news every hour

Once you know your prime suspects, agree with yourself to replace these 'avoiders' with real-life activities (gently and slowly, but surely).

Excerpt from *Ithaka*

When you set out for Ithaka
ask that your way be long,
full of adventure, full of instruction …

And if you find her poor, Ithaka hasn't deceived you.
So wise you have become, of such experience,
that already you'll have understood what Ithaka means.

Constantine Cavafy
(translated by Edmund Keeley)

Practice: Playing with your inner child

Instead of criticizing yourself, look into your heart
for the lonely child, who would prefer playing with
somebody else. You could give yourself a hug and bring
creativity to the foreground of your awareness. Write
down ideas in your notebook.

Is there a friend, neighbour or colleague who might
join you? Maybe you could gently encourage yourself
to try to befriend somebody at your gym or any other
club, even if it is just the receptionist; a friendly face that
recognizes you, and vice versa, will help you get started
and make you feel that you belong.

If, however, your lack of aspiration is due to a fear that
you may not succeed, by either not completing a project
or finding that, on completion, you or others might not
like it, then you need to look for deeper reasons why
completing would have a purpose even if it did not
lead to success. 'Feel the fear and do it anyway.'

Practice: Being your own motivator

Note down in your journal any reasons for completing a task or project, such as:

• Completing this task would improve my skills.
• I would be delighted to have actually done it (and so might … add any names that come to mind).
• It is not always about being the best, but about the adventure of trying something new.
• If others don't like it, they have a right to their opinion. Maybe I will like it, or some will and others won't. (Getting away from 'all or nothing' thinking.)
• Maybe this … is what many people have been waiting for.
• Unless I try, I will never know.
• Everybody fails sometimes; it is part of the human experience. Even if I do fail or do not do as well as I would want to, I will accept and respect myself anyway.
• This project has the potential to help me grow and also learn.

Any of the above reasons are useful, but if one (or two) seems particularly helpful, write it down and stick it onto your computer, noticeboard or fridge.

Earth Teach Me

Earth teach me stillness as the grasses are stilled with light.

Earth teach me suffering as old stones suffer with memory.

Earth teach me humility as blossoms are humble with beginning.

Earth teach me caring as parents who secure their young.

Earth teach me courage as the tree which stands all alone.

Earth teach me limitation as the ant which crawls on the ground.

Earth teach me freedom as the eagle which soars in the sky.

Earth teach me resignation as the leaves which die in the autumn.

Earth teach me regeneration as the seed which rises in the spring.

Earth teach me to forget myself as melted snow forgets its life.

Earth teach me to remember kindness as dry fields weep in the rain.

    Ute prayer, USA

Resisting the 'body cult'

Self-compassion is an important skill, which adds to mindfulness the ability to 'love what is'. If we can learn to truly accept ourselves with compassion, it may be much easier to be present in the 'here and now', and not be drawn to old fears and self-judgement or worries about external appearances.

Living in the 21st century, where, whatever your age, it is widely thought that you should look trim, slim and beautiful, is a constant challenge for most people. This mainly affects women, but men are now also starting to feel the pressure. The author and psychologist Kristin Neff calls it 'the epic struggle to accept our bodies'.

In the UK, the National Health Service (NHS) sources define a person with an eating disorder as somebody who focuses extremely on their weight and body shape, and who makes harmful choices about food and exercising with damaging results to their well-being. The NHS sees about 1 in 250 women and 1 in 2,000 men with a diagnosis of anorexia nervosa at some point in their life. When I was viewing sources and material on the internet,

I came across one plastic surgeon who claimed on the home page of his website to provide 'compassionate, warm, personalized care'.

This phenomenon is not something that has suddenly occurred. All you need to do is watch old black-and-white movies. The actors and actresses were always beautiful in their own way, but men had ordinary bodies, not bulging with muscle, and women came in a variety of shapes and sizes. The more we were able to film and even improve the filmed image, the more 'beauty' became something the ordinary person in the street could not possible achieve. Striving for perfection is no longer just an aspect in the film and photographic industry. But more and more women and men endeavour to look like 'so-and-so' which leads to unhealthy eating patterns and even surgery in order to achieve this goal.

The reality for everybody who thinks their looks must be 'perfect' is the need to use drastic means, including surgery, to get and maintain this look. If these methods

Practice: Self-compassion for the body

This practice has been adapted with permission from the 'Mindful Self-Compassion Program' developed by Chris Germer and Kristin Neff. The goal is to find a balanced way to accept ourselves and our bodies without abusing them by only feeding them over-processed food and unhealthy drinks, and causing ill health by never moving the body (it needs movement) or venturing outdoors.

1　In your notebook, make an honest appraisal of your body, choosing the middle ground. What do you like about your appearance and about how your body functions as a whole? Do you ever give thanks for having feet that can carry you around or for a lovely voice? Really be creative and progress from head to toe.

2　Now, with kindness, write down aspects that are a little less wholesome or, in your view, not pretty enough. Maybe you think your legs are too short, or you have sensitive skin that requires you to put on sun protection, which can be a nuisance. Try to be as objective as you can.

3　Tune into your compassionate heart. Remember how much pressure we are all under to fit the unwritten rules of the media.

4　Maybe you still find it possible to feel gratitude and tenderness for the areas you would prefer to change. Try to figure out whether you *really* need to change something, such as trying a new haircut or hair colour, or maybe just give your body some of the exercise you enjoy and that it longs for. Recall that you are attempting to feel well and content, and that your personal view matters most.

fail, we can now manipulate photographs to achieve the perfect appearance. However, even if you are an ordinary citizen far away from Hollywood, self-acceptance and self-worth are largely dependent on how good-looking you perceive yourself to be.

Whether you are eating too much or too little, whether you feel 'disgusted' with your looks or with your undisciplined behaviour (over-eating, breaking a diet, etc.), self-compassion can help you accept and like yourself just the way you are. Once you achieve this, you will be able to decide – in a more balanced mood – what you really want to eat or drink, and which sport or movement programme you would actually enjoy and therefore stick to. Many people dislike going to the gym, but they may be fine with swimming, walking or practising yoga, Pilates, t'ai chi or chi kung.

8 Compassionate leadership, compassionate living

DO YOU SOMETIMES WONDER WHY you are struggling, why most people seem not to care, and why it is you who can no longer cope with the news of the horrific things that humans do to each other? In those moments of despair and despondency, it really can help to remember that there are men and women who fly high like a white dove in order to see and act on behalf of others.

In the late 1960s, the Buddhist monk Thich Nhat Hanh was travelling though the USA on a journey for reconciliation. The Vietnam War was still in progress, and Thich wanted to share with the regular American what it meant to live in a war zone: what the farmers and their children had to endure because of cruel political manoeuvres. This very gentle, little man had so much kindness and compassion that on most occasions he connected directly with the audience's heart. He talked not about guilt or retribution, but about the daily suffering that occurred so far away that people could easily pretend it was not happening.

He told stories about Christianity and Buddhism, and the simple lives of most people in this region of the world, and soon the audience was mesmerized. His tales spoke of the unforgettable beauty of his homeland, but he did not shy away from mentioning the suffering, manifested in burned houses and bodies, and many orphaned children crying through the nights.

On one particular evening, he gave a talk in a well-to-do suburb of St Louis. The venue was a church. Not too long into the talk, in which Thich had once again begged for kindness and for an end to the war, a large and very angry man started to attack him verbally. He did not beat around the bush, but asked Thich straight out why he was not back home helping his folks rather than giving speeches abroad. Thich took a while to respond. He almost whispered his calm reply. He used the metaphor of a tree and asked the man whether he would water the leaves or the roots of the plant. He then continued to explain that the roots, which needed watering, were right here in this country. So, in order to stop the suffering of his people, he had chosen the only option that seemed viable for him: to travel to the USA and talk to the people there. He completely transformed the anger in the room by answering with so much wisdom, clarity and compassion.

After he finished talking, he suddenly left the room and the church. A friend who had watched this whole story unfold followed him and saw how Thich was panting for air. Thich told him how very upset he was after what the man had said to him. He felt his anger rise, but did not want to explode. So he went into deep and slow breathing in order to reconnect. This totally exhausted him. When his friend asked him why he had not shown his anger – that anger could be good at times – Thich apparently answered: 'I am here to speak for [the] Vietnamese … and have to show them what we can be at our best' (Thich Nhat Hanh, *The Miracle of Mindfulness*, Rider, 1991, page 104).

Maybe you can recall being offended or wronged in the past. When others betray you, or act as false witnesses, it may feel like being stabbed or kicked in the stomach. The initial response may be to hurt them back or to set the record straight, so following the example of Thich Nhat Hanh requires enormous discipline but also deep compassion for humanity as a whole.

Recently, the Burmese politician Aung San Suu Kyi returned to Oxford, where she had studied in the 1960s, for the first time. She probably inherited her deep sense of loyalty towards her people from her father who led Burma (now Myanmar) to independence at the beginning of the 20th century.

Just before she married her British husband Michael Aris in 1971, she sent him a letter which made her position and priorities totally clear; she asked him for one assurance only – that she could go back to Burma should her people need her. In 1988 (when her children were 10 and 14), she went home to her mother who had suffered a stroke. She stayed on in Burma after her

mother's death, where she campaigned for democracy, and was kept under house arrest for many years. She was unable to be with her husband when he was dying of cancer in 1999, which must have been very difficult, as they loved each other very much, and she did not see her children again until 2010. In 1991, she was awarded, in absentia, the Nobel Peace Prize, and in her speech 'Freedom from Fear' she said that it was not power that corrupted people's minds but the fear of losing power. She donated the money she received from the Prize (about US$1.3 million) to fund a trust for health and education in Burma.

There are many others who have also been severely wronged, such as Mahatma Gandhi, His Holiness the 14th Dalai Lama and Martin Luther King, but one thing they had in common was that they overcame fear and spoke their truth. If you can uphold your spirit and your deep conviction in the face of fear and possible death, then speaking with honesty and conviction is a real achievement. The Dalai Lama has on many occasions thanked the Chinese for having given him the gift of 'patience'. In his millennial appeal, he said that we did not need temples, churches, mosques or any other places of worship, but rather we should each endeavour to make our heart and mind into a temple.

An eye for an eye makes the whole world blind.

Mahatma Gandhi (1869–1948)

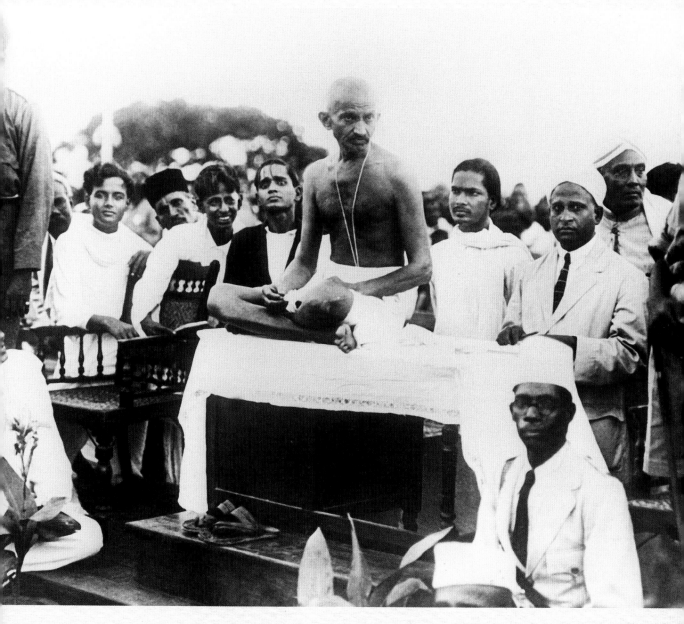

Mahatma Gandhi in Madras, giving a speech before a group of boy scouts, circa 1915.

Practice: A compassionate approach to an argument

Here is a practice that the neuropsychologist Rick Hanson has developed and allowed me to share with you.

1   Start by getting centred, which can take a little while. Feel your feet firmly on the ground and imagine roots coming out of them and deeply connecting you to the earth.

2   Take a few mindful breaths. Give yourself the gift of time.

3   Have compassion for yourself. Feel the pain the other has caused in you. Allow it to be there rather than push it down. Maybe imagine a compassionate being, who loves you, standing right next to you.

4   Ask yourself: what did really happen? Like a referee in a sports match, try to see both sides of the misunderstanding.

5   How bad was the verbal attack or the belittling you experienced? On a scale from 0 to 10 (an angry look is 1; being beaten up and finding yourself in hospital is 10), how bad was it, really? If the event is a 3 on the awfulness scale, why do you experience emotional reactions that are appropriate to a 5 or even higher?

6   See the big picture. Recognize, if at all possible, what was not so bad in the situation. Observe it in the larger context of your life experience. Are there any unrelated good things happening for you, too?

7   Reflect about the other person. Consider the multitude of reasons responsible for their hurtful behaviour. Maybe it was not at all intentional. Even if it was, maybe they had heard incorrect information about you. Try to have compassion for them and yourself. Maybe you need to take responsibility for your own part in the matter. Leave blaming and shaming aside, and try to be as objective as you possibly can. It is possible to experience compassion and forgiveness for others, even if their actions were wrong.

8   For future reference, protect yourself from people who tend to wrong or hurt you; shrink the relationship to a safe size. Get support and have witnesses. Build up your resources. Get good advice from a friend, therapist or lawyer, or even the police. If appropriate, pursue justice.

9   Communicate what needs to be said and make requests for the future. 'If I seem a nuisance to you, could you talk with me directly and explain, please?' 'Could you please not use swear words?' Think of your own requests now, and maybe write them down in your notebook.

10 For your own sake, try to gently release anger and hurt thoughts and feelings. Stop your mind from ruminating about the past, and focus on the here and now. All you can really do is what you have just attempted. Others may respect you for it, or they may not even listen. Many people will act selfishly and disappoint you.

11 Most importantly, find peace in your heart.

Compassionate communication

It happens almost every day – you feel hurt, annoyed and even angry because of other people's thoughtless words or acts. Frequently, you also feel misunderstood by others, but it aches most when you feel your closest friends and family are not 'getting' you. Compassionate communication endeavours to explore why you are misunderstood or misunderstand others. The understanding you can find through the means of compassionate communication can help change the one person you are really responsible for: yourself.

You may want to find out why there are certain patterns in meaningful relationships that cause a breakdown in communication. Once you have explored those patterns, you may want to learn how to change your communication style so that it feeds rather than drains your interactions with others. You may also want to know how good and fruitful communication works in order to create the inner strength to strive for new goals and more meaningful relationships.

In order to become more compassionate when communicating, try the following:

- Explore whether and how often your thinking can be judgemental or blaming of others and of yourself.
- Experiment with empathic listening and speaking, so that you truly learn to hear what others are saying, and others understand you as you would wish to be understood.
- Take time to observe every day the core beliefs (thinking and behaviour life traps) that underlie much of your day-to-day reactive thinking; see how greater familiarity with these beliefs diminishes their impact and makes it possible to replace them, as they are probably no longer helping you.

Der Ton macht die Musik (Using the right tone increases your chance of being heard)

Ancient German proverb

Here is an example. You may have been brought up by parents who, for one reason or another, did not have much time for you. So you learned, in order to survive, that you could only trust yourself and therefore no longer needed others. This insight may have been fine to help you survive your childhood, but if you are still attached to it, you will find it difficult to share thoughts and responsibilities in adult relationships. So you may end up with a very needy partner, or even none at all.

A study at the University of Pittsburgh at Johnstown, called Effects of Variation in Emotional Tone of Voice on Speech Perception, found that 'tone' has a huge impact on how a conversation develops. As our perception always scans for possible dangers, a repeatedly critical, dissatisfied, anxious or judgemental tone can really affect our interactions with others. John Gottman, a leading marriage and parenting researcher, has shown that it may take a handful of positive interactions to make up for a single negative one.

Compassion in the heart and in song

When I was a ten-year-old girl, I was totally fascinated by the Beatles. They were the reason why I chose English as my first foreign language at school. With a dictionary in hand, I would translate their songs into my mother tongue. The Beatle who touched me most was George Harrison. The songs 'Let it Be', 'Yesterday', 'All You Need Is Love', 'Here Comes the Sun' and 'Blackbird' were my favourites. But another part of him was equally compelling as his musical genius, and that was his deep spirituality. Here he touched my soul even more profoundly. Ravi Shankar, the Indian spiritual musician, had become his teacher not only in music but also in matters of the soul. Their friendship, I believe, was one 'made in heaven'. They lived music, and song was their prayer.

George was genuinely connected to the heart, and the language of the heart, and this was more important to him than fame, power or wealth. He was the first top musician to organize a musical event purely to help those who were suffering. He devised the Concert for Bangladesh (1971) to aid the victims of the horrific civil war that involved many atrocities: killings, rape, arson and the ethnic cleansing of Hindus. There was talk of three million deaths and eight or more million people becoming refugees in neighbouring India. Something had to be done, and George arranged it with the help of Ravi Shankar and others. Many musical legends, such as Ringo Starr, Bob Dylan and Eric Clapton, joined him on stage. There were two performances in New York, and the proceeds from these, the records and the documentary film were donated to the refugees and victims of the war.

I feel that George Harrison was a true leader, as he taught hundreds of thousands of people about kindness and compassion. He showed that everybody could actually get involved and lessen the suffering of others.

Practice: Finding compassion through music

I am sure you have a song or a number of songs that you like because they evoke a sense of kindness, togetherness or compassion. Maybe you have never thought about songs in this way. Go to your music collection and see what you can find. Become a compassion researcher. Listen to the music you love and note down in your journal what it is about a song or a melody that touches your heart deeply. What emotions do you feel emerge, what colours or pictures arise in your mind? Maybe you even want to paint a picture and take some photographs that would deepen the story of the song. Let creativity and compassion guide you in your quest.

Dos and don'ts of compassionate communication

(recommended by family therapist and neuropsychologist Rick Hanson):

- Relax your body and heart, as this will soften your speaking tone.
- Avoid using provocative words – exaggerations, accusations, all-or-nothing statements (always, never), insults, swearing, etc.
- Instead, use words that are truthful and not confrontational. Rick says: 'Imagine that you are being video-taped and people you care about will be watching it later; don't say anything you'll regret later.'
- Say what needs to be said. A reasonable and civil tone actually promotes honesty and assertiveness. A softer tone should not replace standing up for yourself.

Compassionate leadership at work

More and more evidence is emerging, including a report in the Journal of Applied Psychology in 2011 entitled *Aggressive Leadership: When Does Strength Become Weakness?* that shows that aggressive, inward-looking leadership in the end neither motivates employees nor helps them to feel part of a bigger picture. What really does work is kindness and compassion on the part of leaders. These instill in the individual the notion of 'we-we' and 'us-us' (rather than 'them-us') and of belonging to a group. Compassion and empathy bring out the best results in companies and the least sickness in employees. Win-win!

In an interview Professor Richard Davidson, of the University of Wisconsin-Madison, stated: 'The manner in which leaders communicate with employees is an essential topic for organizations to recognize.

Communication approaches that leaders apply towards junior employees vary in style, tone, and delivery … Aggressive communication utilized by leadership breaks down the ability for the healthy ebb and flow of conversation to yield productive internal and external responses from the employee.' He explained: 'We have research evidence that shows how positive emotions such as compassion, kindness, inclusivity and praise have absolutely a constructive effect on brain functioning, psychological well-being, physical health, motivation and personal relationships.'

In his book, *It Worked For Me* (Harper, 2012), Colin Powell, the former US Joint Military Chief of Staff and Secretary of State, remembers a childhood experience. His church welcomed an elderly priest who was in

Practice: Sharing compassion as a group

1 Write in your journal about the time you last guided a group you belong to.

2 Which qualities did you share with the other group members that fed and inspired the group? Which ones would you like to let go of?

3 Now set yourself a goal. Step by step, use loving kindness to harness what is wholesome and drop what hinders you and your team.

4 Use sentiments such as: 'May I continue to be patient and praise everyone, however small their contribution may have been' and 'May I show tolerance when [name] gets it wrong and speak kindly when I ask how I could help them overcome this obstacle.'

distress. He says that kindness is not just about being nice; it is also about recognizing another human being who deserves care and respect. Powell is also quoted as saying: 'You can never err by treating everyone in the building with respect, thoughtfulness and a kind word.'

I believe that any group that consists of more than two people is a kind of 'company'. Whether it is a work-related setup, a charity, a family, or friends who pursue a hobby regularly together, whoever leads or guides the unit (even if they take turns) must have the whole group's interests at heart in order for everyone to enjoy the activity and perform their best.

When compassion fills my heart

When compassion fills my heart,
free from all desire,
I sit quietly like the earth.
My silent cry echoes like thunder
throughout the universe.

Jalal al-Din Rumi (1207–1273)

Index

Author's acknowledgements

I want to thank all the wonderful men and women who inspired me to write this guide to self-compassion.

Bernhard, who completely accepts me 'wrinkles and all' and is living a compassionate life.

Helen Stephenson, my friend and co-teacher who is my beacon of light and who shared her ideas with me so generously.

My mum for being so loving in my early years and still loving me with all her heart.

Liz Dean and Sybella Stephens, my editors, who supported me with wise inspiration and patience throughout the project.

My teachers: John Teasdale, Paul Gilbert, Kristin Neff and Chris Germer for passing on their wisdom so kindly and with compassion.

All Beings who have been teachers on this path knowingly or not knowingly.

Photographic credits

Alamy Amana 127; Bernd Mellmann 104–105; George Mayer 12–13; Jim Holden 133; Rafael Ben-Ari 31
Corbis John W Gertz 71; Martin Puddy 118–119; Ocean 52–53; Pete Leonard 55; Radius Images 40–41; Rana Faure 38–39; Stefan Wackerhagen/imagebroker 58–59; Stuart Cox 32–33
Fotolia anitasstudio 2; B and E Dudzinscy 16–17; svedoliver 73; tore2527 18–19
Getty Images Abby Marshall 7 above centre right; Assembly 102–103; Borut Trdina 64–65; Carole Drake 113; Datacraft Co Ltd 10–11; Jamie Grill 35; Jasmina 120–121; Keystone-France 129; Meg Takamura 7 below left; Mitsushi Okada 100–101; Nicky Bond 109; RyanJLane 95; Stepan Popov 29

Glow Images Image Source 138–139; Michael Steines 24–25; Purestock 141; Rashelle Engelbrecht/Anka Agency 80–81
PlainPicture Anna Matzen 99
Shutterstock DwaFotografy 69; Filip Fuxa 48–49; Galyna Andrushko 130–131; iravgustin 79; Kotomiti Okuma 85; Sundari 51; WDG Photo 8–9
SuperStock Image Source 7 below centre; PhotoAlto 42–43; Zen Shui 7 centre left
Thinkstock Comstock 44–45; Hemera 7 above left; iStockphoto 7 below right, 92–93, 116–117; Stockbyte 87